KU-241-550

Other books by Martin Seymour-Smith include:

Literary History and Criticism

Who's Who in Twentieth Century Literature, London and New York, 1976.
Guide to Modern World Literature, London and New York, 1973, rewritten and revised as *MacMillan Guide to Modern World Literature*, 1985.

Biography

Robert Graves: His Life and Work, London and New York, 1982, revised and rewritten, London, 1995.
Rudyard Kipling, London and New York, 1989.
Hardy, London and New York, 1994.

Poetry

Poems (with Rex Taylor and Terence Hards), Dorchester, 1952
Poems, Oxford, 1952.
All Devils Fading, Banalbufar, 1953.
Tea With Miss Stockport, London and New York, 1963.
Reminiscences of Norma, London, 1971.
Wilderness, London, 1995.

Other

Fallen Women, London, 1969.
Sex and Society, London, 1975.

As Editor

Shakespeare's Sonnets, London and New York, 1963, revised and republished 2001.
Ben Jonson's Every Man in his Humour, London and New York, 1964, revised 1979, 1994.

TO THE MEMORY OF ANN WILSON

for whom it was written

Contents

Chronology

6

1899	*Heart of Darkness* is serialized
1900	*Lord Jim*
1902	*Youth*
1903	*Typhoon. Romance* (with Ford), rehearsal for *Nostromo,* published
1904	*Nostromo*
1906	*Mirror of the Sea* (with Ford). Second son, John, born
1907	*The Secret Agent*
1908	*A Set of Six.* Begins quarrel with Ford
1910-11	Without Ford's support, breaks down. Publishes *Under Western* Eyes (1911)
1912	Creative decline begins. A *Personal Record. 'Twixt Land and Sea*
1914	*Chance* sells well, Conrad becomes better off
1915	*Victory. Within the Tides*
1917	*The Shadow-Line* (serialized in previous year)
1919	*The Arrow of Gold*
1920	*The Rescue*
1921	*Notes on Life and Letters*
1923	*The Rover.* Successful visit to United States
1924	Refuses knighthood. Dies

JOSEPH CONRAD

"Man must drag the ball and chain of his individuality up to the end. It is what we pay for the infernal and divine privilege of thought." Joseph Conrad to Marguerite Poradowski, 1894.

"My task appears to me as sensible as lifting the world without that fulcrum which even that conceited ass, Archimedes, admitted to be necessary." Joseph Conrad to Edward Garnett, 19 June 1896.

"Our world of 15 years ago is gone to pieces, what will come in its place, God knows, but I imagine doesn't care... All that survives is 'Excellency a few goats'... esoteric, symbolic, profound and comic." Conrad to Ford, 12 August 1915.

"When Conrad was forthright enough to say that 'all art is autobiographical or it is nothing', he did not mean that all art is biography." Robert Kimbrough in his introduction to *Youth, Heart of Darkness, The End of The Tether, 1984.*

"It is no longer a paradise of snakes. We have brought mankind into it. Mrs Gould, passing on, had the vividness of a figure seen in the clear patches of sun that chequer the gloom of open glades in woods." *Nostromo.*

Coming unexpectedly upon Conrad in London, and seeing him momentarily as a stranger, Ford in *Joseph Conrad* registered this impression: "an old, shrunken, wizened man, in an unbrushed bowler, and ancient burst-seamed overcoat, one wrist wrapped in flannel, the other hand helping him to lean on a hazel walking-stick, cut from a hedge and prepared at home. [He] had in one tortured eye a round piece of dirty window-glass."

"For suffering is the lot of man, but not inevitable failure or worthless despair which is without end – suffering, the mark of manhood, which bears within its pain a hope of felicity like a jewel set in iron" – *Romance,* by Joseph Conrad and Ford Madox Hueffer.

"The only qualification for admission to the pages of the *Review* will be – in the view of the editors – either distinction of individuality or force of conviction, either literary gifts or earnestness of purpose, whatever the purpose may be – the criterion of inclusion being the clarity of diction, the force of the illuminative value of the views expressed. What will be avoided will be the superficiality of the specially modern kind which is the inevitable consequence when nothing but brevity is aimed at. The *English Review* will treat its readers, not as spoiled children who must be amused by a variety of games, but with the respectful consideration due to grown-up minds whose leisure can be interested by something else than the crispness and glitter of popular statement." *Manifesto*, written and agreed by Madox Ford, Arthur Marwood and Joseph Conrad.

" 'As long as I know you understand,' he whispered. 'But of course you do. It's a great satisfaction to have got somebody to understand. You seem to have been there on purpose.' And in the same whisper, as if we two whenever we talked had to say things to each other which were not fit for the world to hear, he added, 'It's very wonderful.' " – Conrad, *The Secret Sharer*.

INTRODUCTORY

It was Ford Madox Hueffer, his collaborator, who first took the full measure of Conrad's genius. On 19 December 1916 Hueffer (in 1919 to change his name to Ford Madox Ford) wrote to him from a military hospital in Rouen. ("C'est fini de moi," he wrote of himself, on account of his lungs and his shell-shock; frequently, he wrote elsewhere, he doubted his sanity). But Ford's voluntary war experiences at the edge of middle-age did not disturb his wisdom or his critical judgement.

Three years previously Conrad had published *Chance,* his first novel to become a best-seller. It marked two turning-points in his career: a too ambitious exploration of his own (in Jungian terms) *anima,* in the person of the heroine, Flora de Barral; it also began his creative decline and commercial success. In 1911 he told his agent, James Bland Pinker – a non-literary but shrewd and often generous man whose business was making money out of books – in a miserably ironic confession (unknown to Ford), that he had given it a 'happy ending' so that it would be 'nicer' for the public. Pinker's heart will have leapt. But, with another irony that his own subtle mind was the first to appreciate, the book's sales also gave him his initial, and sorely-needed, taste of freedom from financial anxiety. Not only did the book itself do well, but the public, especially in America, began to buy his earlier, superior work.

Ford was always inclined to be generous to Conrad, even though the latter eventually rejected him as a close friend. This was in part because he was aware of his own immense debt to him. As we shall see, Conrad's stories, *The End of the Tether* and, most particularly, *The Secret Sharer* reveal, among other matters, both the extent of his debt to Ford, and the real (inner) loss to him of his close companionship. Conrad was never one to fail to compensate posterity for his self-centredness – even if it had not itself had to suffer it.

Ford wrote in his letter from Rouen:

> I have been reading – rather deliriously – *Chance* since I have been in this nice kind place. The end is odd, you know, old boy. It's like a bit of Maupassant tacked onto a Flaubert façade.

> Pardon me if that sounds inept: I think still a good deal about these things – but not cleverly! – And one lives under the shadow of GF [Gustave Flaubert] here. After all you began yr. literary career here – and I jolly well nearly ended mine here

too – And I assure you I haven't lost a jot of the immense wonder at the immensities you bring onto paper. You are a blooming old Titan, really – or do I mean Nibelung? At any rate even in comparatively loose work like *Chance* there is a sense of cavernous gloom, lit up by sparks from pickaxes.

Everything written here was true. Indeed, Ford, as well as being the only person ever trusted by Conrad to write passages into his own work (some of *Heart of Darkness*, fifteen, probably more, pages of *Nostromo*, a half-share of *A Mirror of the Sea*, and much else, are Ford's), understood him better than anyone else has, either before or since – he was, as Conrad tacitly acknowledged, his 'secret sharer'.

Conrad was indeed a 'titanic' novelist by any standards, and *Chance* was certainly 'loose'; it did indeed mark the beginning of a decline which is undeniable (though, as will become apparent, both the extent and the exact course of it are debatable). Yet it did, too, contain much of the old, supreme, Conrad, of the Pole who, in English, only his third language, did indeed light up a 'cavernous gloom' with 'sparks from pickaxes', did illuminate the heart of human darkness with flashes of insight. Conrad, again without Ford's knowledge, wrote to Galsworthy just after he had read the good reviews given to *Chance*, "Now I can't even pretend I am elated. If I had *Nostromo*, *The Nigger* or *Lord Jim* in my desk or only in my head I would feel differently no doubt." No writer knew himself better; but Ford knew him as well. After 1908 or thereabouts he had not been prepared to allow for Ford's presence any longer in his life. He had long known his fate to become one of the supreme writers of fiction; and had therefore known, too, that he was perpetually in danger of falling from that status. No writer can know, to the horror of his self-esteem, that he is one of the best – without knowing, too, what it is like (so equally horribly) not to be. Ford, on the other hand, never wrote to please readers; his own weakest work sprang from sheer exhaustion.

Confronted with an intimate knowledge of an integrity of Ford's alarming kind, Conrad could not but bow out. He understood it too well. The very deficiency of character which was induced in Ford by his own truly ludicrous integrity – his inability to conduct himself either respectably or successfully in this world – gave Conrad uneasy reason to reject him, and to turn to lesser men as anchors. To emphasise his feelings of humiliation, he owed the penniless young Ford money! Yet Conrad had often done so, and (in 1908) he still did. (It may never have been paid back.) It is not a coincidence that, *Under Western Eyes*, his last unequivocally good book, has betrayal as one of its main themes.

Could Ford's verdict – made in late 1916, written when he was himself at the end of his tether, and badly in need of an affection and support which could no longer be forthcoming – have been better stated? No novelist, who was not also a major poet, has scooped so deeply and so courageously into himself for demons acknowledgeably his own, as Conrad did. Perhaps no novelist's stories and novels lend themselves more aptly to the kind of analysis usually applied to poems. There is no more 'perfect' novel than *The Good Soldier*, by the existentially bumbling Ford. Conrad could not reach this technical peak (although he neared it in *The Secret Agent*), but he outdid Ford in power and dramatic tension.

After his death, Conrad's standing went down quite badly, despite the devotion of a few critics, such as Ford himself and Conrad's loyal young friend Richard Curie. The reason for this was in part that his reputation became engulfed by the modernist movement. Indeed, a good deal of recent criticism has spent much time in trying to demonstrate that he was really a modernist or that he anticipated modernism. But he is so interesting in himself, having been – in the historical terms of literary criticism – a genuinely transitional figure, that the exercise of classifying, rather than examining, his work has been largely wasteful.

After 1930, when Gustave Morf's pioneering and eventually highly influential study – insisting upon Conrad's essential Polishness – appeared, there was nothing of consequence until J. D. Gordan's book of 1941. From that time onwards, gradually, Conrad has returned to favour. Recent years have seen a plethora of biographies and studies. His reputation is now established as it never was in his lifetime. It is no more likely to fade than is Stendhal's, another novelist whose fame as a classic did not spread until after his death.

How, and why, did Conrad, the Pole who was a "more English than the English" novelist, who first saw England at the age of twenty-one, the seaman (before that) of an inland country, achieve this in a language (he spoke it with a pronounced accent, with for example a 'dat' for a 'that', for the whole of his life) which he never knew perfectly, and could not even dare to do? Why and how do the most powerful books – by no means forgetting the shorter fiction – of this chronicler of 'glamour' and 'adventure', of crime in Africa, revolution in South America, terrorism in London, assassination and intrigue in Russia, grow inexorably inwards? They become inimitably dark and yet heroic records of journeys into the interior of the human heart, incomparably exciting examinations of the propensities and motives of human beings to become solitary criminals. They are beautifully agitating explorations of people's paradoxical need to be, simultaneously, members of communities and yet so alone as to be able to understand the need to create a world where there is no world – to make a world out of emptiness. One of the prime meanings of 'the double', a theme Conrad explored, is that one twin is individual, the other – identical – *is of the species.* The irony of it all was that, as Conrad knew, the world when imagined out of a truly earned emptiness – a genuine compassion, and an aching care for all fellow human beings – must always turn out to be no less than a paradise whose beauty cruelly derives from the brutal and narcissistic experience of 'ordinary reality': as if Plato's 'forms' themselves did not lie behind their tainted shadows, but were inspired by, owed their being to, those very shadows. That was what Rilke, writing at much the same time, had meant when in his first Duino Elegy he wrote the lines (relevant in particular to Conrad's quest): *Denn das Schöne is nichts/als des Schrecklichen Anfang, den wir noch grade ertragen,/und wir bewundern es so, weil es gelassen verschmäht,/uns zu zerstoren.* (For the Beautiful is nothing but the first feeling of the Terrible, which we are still able, barely, to endure – and we admire it so much, because it serenely disdains to destroy us.)

Who was this strange writer? What made him?

I THE LIFE

Józef Teodor Natlecz Korzeniowski was born on 3 December 1857, at a manor leased by his father, Apollo Korzeniowski, and his worshipped wife Ewa Bobrowska. His childhood was so wretched – but by political circumstance rather than parental cruelty or stupidity – that he spent his life, at an unconscious level, trying to disown it. The Manor of Derebczynka stood some hundred miles from Kiev at Berdichev, in Podolia – now the independent Ukraine, but then a southern province of Poland, which was clumsily, cruelly and uncomprehendingly ruled by Russia, whose governments conveniently believed that the Poles needed only to be made into proper Slavs to be able to understand their proper destiny. Even the Russian language was imposed upon them, although Joseph Conrad was never to know that language well.

Apollo's profession was manager of agricultural estates, his status 'landed gentry'; but he reserved his real energies for his stand against Russian domination, and for his writing: 'a Marxist without Marx' (but very much with Tolstoy), he wrote cycles of poems which lamented the failure of the 1848 revolution, and celebrated a revolt of Ukrainian peasants of 1855, novels, translations (Shakespeare, Dickens, Hugo), and criticism. Although worthy, his works were unoriginal, and have failed to survive. Yet, as has been suggested, the son's writings can be shown to parallel the father's in an uncanny way – almost as if he wanted to make them good, and to make good come from them. It can never be forgotten that Conrad always regarded his parents as martyrs to Russian imperialism.

Thus he was, throughout his life, to loathe not only Russia, but, sometimes disproportionately – as in the famous case of the Dostoievski to whom, particularly in the *Secret Agent* and *Under Western Eyes*, he was so indebted – Russian writers. Apparently non-political, eagerly desiring to attend to what he called his own "business", he could not avoid an anti-imperialist stance. But he saw revolution as futile.

Apollo was arrested by the Russians in 1861 and after imprisonment in Warsaw exiled to the Russian city of Vologda. His and his wife's health broke under the strain, and they both contracted tuberculosis. Ewa died in 1865 and, although father and son were then allowed to move back to Poland, to Cracow, Apollo followed her in 1869.

Joseph, now twelve, became the ward of his maternal uncle, Tadeusz Bobrowski, a wealthy landowner to whom, for his generous and enlightened, though frequently severe, support during the years of his adolescence, he owed much. Tadeusz died in 1894, and Conrad's first novel is dedicated to his memory. Of four more uncles, two died, one was imprisoned, and a fourth was exiled to Siberia. As a boy Conrad was unusually widely read, even then (as always) seeking, as he put it in the essay "Tales of the Sea", "fidelity to experience". He early attached importance to such authors as Fenimore Cooper (for his sea tales) and Marryat, both of whom he read in translation. Shakespeare, Dickens, de Vigny and Hugo he knew from his father's own translations. He became acquainted with Cervantes at an early age. Between the ages of thirteen and seventeen he travelled in Europe with his tutor, Adam Marek Pulman. He was a very highly strung youth, and, wishing above all to get away from Poland and its associations, and to avoid being conscripted for service in the Russian army, quit his studies in Cracow, in 1874, to become an apprentice sailor in Marseilles. He was so identified with Poland, with his own crushed Polishness, and with his (hardly unjustified) notion of the murder of his parents by Russians, that he felt he would perish, intellectually or even physically – just as they had – if he remained. And it must be recognised that this Russian imperialism, like the other imperialisms, was a great injustice.

Conrad, by the time he arrived at Marseilles, was almost eighteen. His long affair with the sea resembled, in essence, all his other really important affairs – with the women he loved, with his English wife (and nurse) Jessie, with his own work, with Ford – a love-hate relationship. He had an outer circle of friends, consisting of such as John Galsworthy and Edward Garnett, of whom he was fond and to whom he was loyal, but whom he used (almost if not quite unscrupulously) for money and for the support, profound though he knew very well it was not, without which he knew he could neither live or work. His complex relationship, begun in 1906, with the liberal and humane Tory lawyer Arthur Pierson Marwood, an original for Ford's Christopher Tietjens of the tetralogy *No More Parades*, and of the Edward Ashburnham of his *The Good Soldier*, was exceptional.

In Marseilles Conrad mastered the elements of seamanship – and his second language, French. He joined the French marine service. He read Flaubert, always his first master, and other French novelists and poets. He became the dandy which, as a seaman, he would always seem, ran up huge debts, flirted with Carlist conspirators, engaged in gun-running when bureaucracy denied him naval work, and started to learn English in earnest. In the course of all this he met (1876) the Corsican adventurer Dominic Cervoni, who provided him with much copy, and in particular with the original for *Nostromo*. Had he continued to work for the French merchant navy he would have been liable for Russian military service (of up to twenty-five years, no less, as the son of a 'convict'). He engaged in a love affair, lost all he had in a gambling venture in Monte Carlo, and indulged himself in a decidedly risky para-suicide. But to what extent he fictionalised this desperate and make-or-break period, of the first months of 1878, is a matter of conjecture, and is variously treated by his biographers. In *The Arrow of Gold* he romanticised the events of that year; but by then he had become exhausted by illnesses, his powers had declined, and so he produced an entertainment, even a fantasy 'romantic' in the wrong sense, the sense in which his best fiction is so at odds to deny – rather than an analysis or even an examination of them.

The details are scant. Certainly his long-suffering uncle, not as open in his Polishness as Apollo had been, upbraided him for his over-prolific use of his allowance; nor was he ever to be particularly scrupulous, in an orthodox sense, about how he raised money. He was never quite dishonest; but he had a disrespect for high finance, and actually believed it smacked of dishonesty. Millionaires, he felt, were "the real anarchists". During the years of his best writing he earned little, and had to borrow prodigally – or to obtain grants from the Royal Literary Fund – to keep his wife and two sons afloat. The award of a civil list pension, arranged for him by William Rothenstein and Edmund Gosse, in 1905, made things a little easier. There were many cynical schemes in those years, mostly unsuccessful, for raising money through such things as insurance policies. The poverty in which he was kept now makes painful reading – yet, as everyone agrees, he seemed to work best under such barely endurable pressures.

By the April of 1878 he was in England. On April 4 he sailed in his first British ship, the *Mavis*, a 764-ton steamer, to Constantinople. There were many more voyages. In November 1886 he passed examination which qualified him as a captain in the British merchant marine, and in the same year became a naturalised British citizen; within a few years of that he was calling himself Joseph Conrad. He only very gradually learned English, and, naturally enough, always remained anxious about his use of it.

The beginning of Conrad's career as a senior sailor was fraught with difficulties. When, with much sea experience behind him, he first took his master's examination in the late July of 1886 he failed; but he kept this from his uncle – and avoided the subject in his letters to him until he was able to pass. He never forgot the humiliating secret he had to keep from one upon whom he felt dependant, and, as his biographer Karl well puts it, was "already entering into the experience of so many of his protagonists who carry with them great secrets, men who move silent for fear their privileged knowledge will become revealed to a public for whom they feel contempt". Conrad would always feel contempt for the readers who simply formed 'the market'; and he would always be aware that the 'knowledge' he carried was, in its own way, as esoteric and as psychologically dynamic as an ancient gnostic teaching. Until *Chance* he only intermittently allowed the requirements of this market to deter him from his purpose, although he was highly susceptible to suspicions that he had compromised himself in some way. It is not surprising that in the end he gave part way under the strain. But he respected his individual readers in a way that he could not respect commercial fiction, the market (or even, as he frequently complained, his agent Pinker).

Though Conrad, after his oats had been fully sown in 1878, was often land-bound, and had difficulty in obtaining satisfactory berths, he did sail extensively: in the Mediterranean, the South China Seas, the Indian Ocean and the Pacific. He gained most of his nautical expertise on sailing vessels – and this just at the time when sail was giving way to steam. In 1887 he was injured aboard the *Highland Forest*, and had to be hospitalised in Singapore. In the following year he got to know the Malay archipelago well, while serving as officer on the *Velar*. In 1888 he was master of the *Otago* – his only command, from which he resigned in the following year. He passed through most of the trials and dangers which are the lot of the sailor. He was to make the fullest use of these experiences, just as he was – but much more obliquely in the best than in the final works – of those more wildly 'romantic' ones he had had as a very young man.

An ill-conceived voyage up the Congo River in 1890, undertaken for an unscrupulous Belgian trading company, Société Anonyme pour le Commerce du Haut-Congo, was responsible for *Heart of Darkness*, the grimmest (and most celebrated) of his short novels. But this tale, describing a part of what he called the "vilest scramble for loot that ever disfigured the history of human conscience and geographical exploration" – his comment on the Belgian exploitation of the Congo – permanently depressed him, damaged his health and gave him an absolute distaste for any kind of politics. He was from 1890 (in which year he became thirty-three) often on the edge of outright invalidism; his chief complaints being that type of arthritis called gout, and malaria. For Conrad, most of his ailments were 'gout': gout of the stomach, gout of the throat, and all sorts of other 'gout', as well as the painful swelling of joints which is called gout today. In essence he and his doctors were probably right, and his problems did arise from a single cause – which might as well be called 'gout'. And gout is an eminently psychosomatic disease. His prospects as a captain became fewer, and after two voyages on the *Torrens* (1891-93) as first mate, during the second of which he met Galsworthy – to whom (wrote Galsworthy), he "told of life, not literature" – he said goodbye to the sea. He was only to make one more voyage, an aborted one as it turned out, on the *Adowa*, as second mate, over the Christmas of 1893. He had met Jessie George in the autumn of 1893.

By then he had what would be his first novel, *Almayer's Folly*, half completed. He had started it in the margins of his copy of *Madame Bovary*. He was sick and without prospects. Political despair had driven him into his role as a sailor, now physical illness drove him, though he was reluctant, into that of, not just writer, but major writer. His ambition was so boundless that he did not even have to consider its nature – but this ambition had in its sights not success, but the discovery of meaning in life. He well understood what fate had in store for him – the role of major writer – and was determined to live that evil fate to the full. He had to get on with it. He was almost thirty-six. The year 1894 was crucial for him: he finished and re-wrote *Almayer's Folly*, had it accepted by Fisher Unwin ("an Israelite interested only in money," he later called him), started a new story, *An Outcast of the Islands*, and began his friendship in earnest with the editor Edward Garnett. (Conrad's animadversions towards Jews could never have been made had he known of later developments, though he did confuse Jews with commercialism; ignorant of their history, he was never a fully-fledged Jew-baiter in the style of a Pound or an Eliot – he later wrote, "I trust I have no contemptible prejudices against any kind of human beings"). Conrad was probably never in 'romantic love' with Jessie; but of course he came to love and appreciate her in a different way. We see his exasperation with her stupidity in the portrait of Winnie Verloc in *The Secret Agent* – but of course Jessie 'is' not Winnie Verloc any more than Conrad 'is' himself the pornographer, spy and informer Verloc.

The comparison of Conrad's life as sailor with his life as writer, two different kinds of voyage, may seem so trite as to be not worth making. But such a comparison, in his case, is in danger of being so obvious as to be missed. The sailor's voyage is through and around what lies outside himself, and, for the intelligent and sensitive one, is redolent of a journey within. Conrad's father had been a failed writer; both his father and his mother had died because of unjust, humanly needless, misguided, oppression. It can seem, it may very well be, that the first part of his life, as seaman, was no more than a semi-conscious preparation for the final part. The boy, cut off from his mother at eight, and from his father at twelve, already spellbound by books, enters the arena of action in order, in a future certain only in the nature of its exact aim, to recollect it in a meaningful way. Rebelliousness is gallant and morally justified, but suicidal in an evil world. Could it be transformed into purposeful action on the sea? His parents' bleak experience, his wild youth of gambling and quasi-criminal action, what he saw in the Congo: all this and much else taught him that revolution was quite as doomed as it was desirable, that he must try to transform his despair. After all, his attempt at suicide – when he shot himself in the chest, but gambled on fair odds that he would fail – had failed. His uncle did then pay off his debts! He had been asking himself a question: 'Am I good enough?' Alas for his happiness, he was; and his recovery from his wound – an affair about which he was of course particularly 'secret', and which he rationalised as the result of a duel – told him so. By the end of 1897, he thought he saw the meaning of it all, and told his friend, the always sympathetic and intelligent Cunninghame Graham, that the "mysteries of the universe do not concern us in the least. The fate of a humanity condemned to perish from cold is not worth troubling about... we don't know what forgiveness is, nor what is love, nor what God is"; a week or two earlier he had declared that he would admit that "to look at the remorseless process is sometimes amusing". But that remark was characteristic of his then maturing irony: what his work ultimately shows us is, not only a superbly educated bleakness of mind, but a search for hope, since we cannot speak of our lack of understanding of exquisite qualities, such as forgiveness and love, if we do not know very well that they do after all exist – "we do not know where God is" means what it says; but it also means, *God is somewhere*. We misread Conrad if we fail to remember this.

Necessity was by now causing him, as he put it in a letter, to "begrudge every minute" he spent "away from paper". When his first novel was published, it was met with praise from an anonymous H.G. Wells and most other reviewers, one of whom believed that the world would soon know "a new great writer". He knew about that, and took it for granted. Kipling told us of how he, too, knew his destiny, and of how he also knew that he only had to "play his cards". But ultimately Kipling did not play his hand very well; or perhaps it was not that good a hand (although good enough for the Nobel Prize which eluded the too pessimistic Pole – the prizes, endowed by a purveyor of dynamite, were for long supposed to be awarded to hopeful types). Conrad, hardly one to fall into any kind of Kiplingesque imperialism, found his superb cards infinitely more difficult to play – every minute of the game was anguish to him, as his letters amply testify. In August 1897, incidentally, Conrad wrote (to Graham) of Kipling (whose success both worried and fascinated him) that he had the "the wisdom of the passing generations" and held this "in perfect sincerity". He continued, with an ironic, yet half-appreciative contempt:

> Some of his work is in impeccable form and because of that little thing he shall sojourn in hell only a very short while. He squints with the rest of his excellent sort. It is a beautiful squint; it is a useful squint. And – after all – perhaps he sees around the corner? And suppose Truth is just around the corner like the elusive and useless loafer it is? I can't tell. No one can tell. It is impossible to know. It is impossible to know anything tho' it is possible to believe a thing or two… I judge the man in his time – and space. It is a small space.

Almayer's Folly, a tale about an avaricious Dutch merchant in the Malayan port of Sambir, is not one of his best novels; but as 'prentice work it is of the highest order. Its successor and sequel, *An Outcast of the Islands*, is, however, by comparison, a weak performance, and less assured in its use of English. But with *The Nigger of the "Narcissus"*, a complex story of a storm off the Cape of Good Hope, and of an enigmatic black sailor, a kind of gloss on Coleridge's *Ancient Mariner*, he suddenly showed his genius almost to the full.

Meanwhile, after being romantically involved with two other women, Conrad married Jessie George in March 1896. ("Look here, my dear," he told her, "we had better get married and out of this. Look at the weather. We will get married at once and get over to France. How soon can you be ready? In a week – a fortnight?") She could share none of his artistic aspirations: "for all her good and gentle qualities, she could not be consulted on artistic matters, nor could she ever be", writes Karl. But she had her woman's intuitions, so that Karl's judgement, while true on the surface, is distortingly unfair. She did not understand his writings (she was beaten up by his writing of them, though, however magnificent they undoubtedly are to others), and he probably chose her because there was never a chance of that – and also simply because he did not want, and could not stand, a real critic right by his side. He was not to be able to endure Ford for very long. Although Jessie's own health – from 1904, when she injured her knees –

became distressingly poor and disabling, almost as poor as his, she provided Conrad with much of the sort of domestic help he required, as well as two sons. At first they lived in Essex, but quite soon moved to Kent, in which county – at a number of different addresses, and with a short interlude in Bedfordshire – they settled for good.

It was at this point that Conrad found he needed a mentor besides Edward Garnett: one who possessed the imagination and the creative know-how which the good but limited Garnett lacked. Garnett also had the disadvantage that he greatly admired Russians – his wife Constance busily translated them and made them familiar to English readers – and revolutionaries. Conrad at first, rather blunderingly, tried to find this mentor in the American writer Stephen Crane, author of *The Red Badge of Courage*, who had come to live near him (at Brede, in East Sussex, near Rye and the county border with Kent). Crane influenced *The Nigger*, and this was noted at the time; but Crane was already too ill, and the ideas of collaboration which the two men discussed did not work out. Crane died in the Black Forest in 1900.

After that Conrad may have vaguely thought of his friend the Scottish writer and left-wing politician R. B. Cunninghame Graham, a vigorous essayist and story and travelwriter, as some kind of systematic mentor. The red-haired and flamboyant Graham, an early opponent of capital punishment, founder with Keir Hardy of the Scottish Labour Party, had had the ironic courage to call an impenitent thief humanly superior to various sorts of socially respectable thieves such as bankers and lawyers who had been caught and who then tried to exonerate themselves. He had done two honourable months in prison for having – while an MP on "Bloody Sunday" in 1887 – led an attack on the police in Trafalgar Square. But Conrad knew that Graham had a faith in human nature which his much more ruthless delving into his own nature permanently denied him. Besides, he could never have collaborated with Cunninghame Graham. The circumstances were against it. He was much under the spell of Henry James, but James was, of course, as much beyond his reach as he was of anyone else's. So, after some consultation with W. E. Henley and with Edward Garnett himself, he chose Ford, then himself only just finding his feet, but with more experience of the literary world, and already possessed of his astonishing know-how – to advise and help him. In his generous way, Ford had more faith in human nature than his older friend; but that faith was expressed with a unique irony in which Conrad could joyfully share. It admiringly awarded him a shard of crazy idealism which he could just endure. One famous anecdote, which has furrowed the brows of many critics, is revealing of the nature of what they shared. In their first collaboration, *Romance*, Ford gave to an obscure peasant character these lines in answer to a judge's question as to his occupation:

> "Excellency – a few goats..."

Ford wrote:

> No sooner had [I] got the words on paper than Conrad burst into one of his roars of ecstasy. "This," he shouted when he was in a condition to speak, "is genius!"

Although the editor of an anthology of Ford's letters, an American academic, managed rather grimly to discern that the peasant's answer is 'evasive', he also thought that Conrad's 'delight' was 'inexplicable'. That bafflement, alas, was not genius. Vital literature (like the minds of Poles under Russian domination), is often about the common man concealing his private affairs from the 'superior authorities'; it is about freedom – about people rather than about the inert souls who never wholly succeed in ruling them; about 'how to fill in forms'.

Conrad's offer to collaborate with Ford on a novel which it was known he could not get on with, was a gesture difficult to make for so extremely proud a man. But Conrad made it, his inner creative needs knowing that he needed a true companion. He knew himself, and so he wrote to Henley, in October 1898, uneasily, that

> It never entered my head [meaning that it had loomed so large that he had overlooked it] that I could be dangerous to Hueffer in the way you point out. The affair [of collaborating with him on the book, then called *Seraphina*, which became their joint *Romance*] had a material rather than an artistic aspect for me. It would give – I reflected – more time to Hueffer for tinkering at his verses: for digging, hammering, chiselling or whatever process by which that mysterious thing – a poem – is shaped out of that barren thing – inspiration. As for myself I meant to keep the right to descend into my own private little hell – whenever the spirit moved me to do that foolish thing – and produce alone from time to time – verbiage no doubt – my own – and therefore very clear .... No, I shall not go mad and bite him, at least not without a fair warning...

This was hardly ingenuous: to pretend that Ford was primarily a poet, and then state that Ford would now have time, in that role, to do what Conrad wanted him to help him with – to chisel and hammer out and make lucid the heavy stuff from his unconsciousness. He had already met Ford (in the February, or the May – the most likely date – or at the very latest in September 1898), and he had seen instantly what sort of man he was and what sort of intimate companion he could be – and so he already knew that Ford had the generosity to be his pilot, as the tale *The End of the Tether* recognises: in it, the blind Whalley (a pun on 'whale' – which needs a pilot-fish. It also represents, at a certain level, Conrad 'blind' as a writer in English) is saved by his pilot Serang (in French as *seran(coir)* suggesting *hackle*, comber-out), a near homophone of 'seraphic', the leader of an East Indian crew of Lascars – but skipper of his own "small native boat", with all the mysteries of that.

Initially the two men proved symbiotic, sharing the same sense of irony, the same sense of humour, the same lack of money, and – despite their temperamental differences – the same outlook on life. Later Conrad would reject Ford. The story *Secret Sharer*, a fable of what too close friendship entails, explores the nature of their relationship. There is no doubt that Conrad became profoundly dependent on his friend, collaborator (and even banker) – and that he resented this. Ford and his wife Elsie were living at Pent Farm, in the remote village of Postling, near Lympne; soon Conrad and Jessie took it over, as Ford's tenants; they remained there until 1907. The lonely road and the quiet farmhouse there, hardly touched by modernity and 'progress', are still redolent of their friendship, of *Nostromo*, of *The Secret Agent*.

The two men collaborated in three novels, *The Inheritors, Romance* and, later, *The Nature of a Crime* – and Ford is known to have written some of the work Conrad published as his own. He was the only man Conrad ever so trusted, and at the height of their friendship their artistic intimacy was perhaps as intense as any that has ever been achieved amongst two major writers. It was Ford above all who helped Conrad to realise the aim he had set forth in his preface to *The Nigger of the "Narcissus"*: "My task which I am trying to achieve is, by the power of the written word, to make you hear, to make you feel – it is, before all, to make you see". This, combined with his Flaubertian anxiety to make "every line" "carry its justification", offers the essential key to Conrad's aspirations as an writer.

Conrad, with Ford's encouragement, and with his cooperation, now entered into the most creatively fruitful period of his life. After the five stories in *Tales of Unrest*, he wrote *Lord Jim*, *Typhoon*, his undisputed masterpiece *Nostromo*, *The Secret Agent* and *Under Western Eyes*. Critical opinion is still divided, and will remain so, about the worth of the successors to this bumper crop. Some assert that *Under Western Eyes* is worthy to rank with the masterpieces, others that it shows a falling-off. There is more agreement about *Chance*, the novel with which Conrad at last reached the reading public in quantity: this is a botched novel, in some eyes 'feminist' (but it is odd that the same critics do not see feminism in the creation of the great Mrs Gould of *Nostromo*), and containing in any case both good and bad elements, themes peculiar to the author and, simultaneously, concessions to the marketplace. But little that Conrad wrote – and all he did write bears the mark of great pain and anxiety – lacks some touch of genius.

Lord Jim is (except for the 13,000-word story *Youth*) the first of his books to be narrated by Charlie Marlow, the English sailor whose complex function, for Conrad, was as mixture, or even blend, of storyteller, self-critic, reader, and, above all, English gentleman Conrad wanted to be but knew he could never really become. Nothing much therefore in Conrad's fiction can actually concern Marlow beyond his experience as onlooker (but that is considerable) and, later, narrator. In *Lord Jim* Marlow acts, in addition to his habitual functions, as father-figure to the unhappy eponymous hero, who, having deserted the passengers on a ship he mistakenly believed to be sinking, spends the rest of his life in trying to atone. There Marlow became an English Conrad coddling the lost Pole Conrad. In *Lord Jim* his writing is not at its best: he counterpoints romanticism with sceptical realism, but never resolves the balance. It remains a major novel about a cowardly act, and its consequences for a man of conscience.

Heart of Darkness, a short novel, which originally comprised the middle section of the collection *Youth*, tells the story of a nightmare journey up the Congo River to retrieve Kurtz, a seemingly enlightened Belgian trader who has become murderously insane. It is by no means well written in all its parts: the use of vague words such as 'inscrutable' and 'inconceivable' has been much criticised, and this obfuscating rhetoric, though mainly owing to Conrad's difficulties with English, does amount to a major flaw in the tale, whose power, though undoubted, only uneasily transcends it. It captured the imagination of later twentieth-century writers such as T. S. Eliot, who used a phrase from it as an epigraph to the original of his poem *The Waste Land* (but was dissuaded by Pound from printing it): although, in Lionel Trilling's words, it had no "manifest polemical intention", it "contains in sum the whole of the radical critique of European civilisation that has been made by literature in the years since its publication".

Nostromo, usually considered to be Conrad's greatest novel, was originally serialised. It offers, together with *The Secret Agent*, an ample refutation of the oft-repeated charge that Conrad's politics were 'reactionary' (one of the closest of his friends, after all, was the revolutionary socialist jailbird, R. B. Cunninghame Graham). Conrad's politics were neither reactionary nor 'left-wing': he simply attended, as he declared, to "his business". He saw things as they are. This is why he is 'our contemporary'. *Nostromo* extends the critique of modern political life begun in *Heart of Darkness*, and, in the character of Mrs Gould, creates one of the most memorable of all fictional demonstrations of feminist convictions. In it Conrad invents the imaginary South American country of Costaguana (literally Shitcoast), in the midst of a revolution which he demonstrates is doomed to failure. Besides Mrs Gould, victim of her husband's greed, the novel is full of memorable characters: Decoud, the dandy who dedicates himself to a sacrifice in which he is too empty even to believe, the greedy Charles Gould and, above all, the ex-Garibaldian captain of the dock-workers himself, Nostromo, simultaneously hero and traitor.

In terms of technique, *The Secret Agent*, a grimly satirical, often comic, account of a group of shabby anarchists and their equally shabby pursuers – policemen and holders of high office – is Conrad's most finely wrought novel. Here he expiates his own guilt feelings by examining himself in the person of Verloc, pornographer and grubby double-agent, and his wife in the person of Winnie Verloc, who torments her husband with her silence. This novel is, wrote Albert J. Guerard, "a small and symmetrical triumph of controlled form". The exhausted and sick Conrad, tortured by gout and subject to recurrent depressions, did not achieve another novel at this high level; although most of the later novels do have their champions, the consensus is overwhelmingly that after *The Secret Agent* he lost power. *Under Western Eyes* (this operates at only just under the power of *The Secret Agent*) apart, the strongest case can be made out for the very late *The Shadow Line* (1917), written (significantly) as a tribute to his son Borys, who, along with so many other young men, was suffering as a soldier in World War I (which, happily, he survived). Borys was born in 1898, his more unequivocally 'English' brother John eight years later.

Under Western Eyes, a surprisingly Dostoievski-like novel for one who made such a loud profession of his loathing of all things Russian, is a tale of guilt and betrayal amongst Russian revolutionaries in Geneva. It is flawed only by its too great debt to Dostoievski's *Crime and Punishment* and *The Devils* and by its recourse to extreme melodrama. But the close study of Razumov, the student responsible for the torture and murder of his colleague, amounts to great literature. There are similar, but much weaker, elements in *Chance* and *Victory*. The final romances are interesting solely because they came from the pen of one who had once been a great writer, and because they cast some vague light on aspects of his early life. After he finished *Under Western Eyes* he suffered a severe breakdown and was never the same after it.

Conrad returned to Poland in 1914, an inauspicious time. He was almost trapped there by the outbreak of the 1914-18 War, but managed to get back by August 1914. He gained the good friendship of the loyal and decent young man Richard Curle, who was just as intelligently traditional in his views, and untroubled by creative gifts, as Conrad needed. His health gradually worsened. In 1923 he enjoyed a trip to America during which he was fully honoured. On 3 August 1924, not long after refusing a knighthood, he died at his house, Oswalds, at Bishopsbourne, near Canterbury.

II THE MAJOR WORKS (1)

The years between 1897 and 1911 are commonly regarded as Conrad's major phase. The cases for *Chance* and *Victory* , as wholes, being equal to the novels of that period have not been convincingly made. Therefore the main space in this survey has been given to discussions of the volumes *The Nigger of the "Narcissus"* (1897), *Youth* (published in 1902 and consisting of *Youth*, 1897, *Heart of Darkness*, 1899 – these two first appeared in *Blackwood's Magazine* – and *The End of the Tether*), *Lord Jim* (1900), *Typhoon* (published in 1903 with four other stories), *Nostromo* (1904), *The Secret Agent* (1907), *Under Western Eyes* (1911) and *'Twixt Land and Sea* (published in 1912 and continuing "The Secret Sharer"). Other short fiction by Conrad, in particular *The Shadow-Line* (1917), which is the best of his later work (and something of an interruption of his decline) are more cursorily discussed. A relatively long discussion of "The Secret Sharer" has been undertaken because its psychological roots are crucial to Conrad's life and its meaning, and because it demonstrates particularly clearly how his creative imagination functioned – especially as it was then, at almost its last gasp.

It should be said at the outset that Conrad's quite undeniable faults include passages of extreme meretriciousness, when he was writing potboilers such as *Chance* (or, earlier, when he was ill, late with copy and so simply forced to lapse by domestic necessity, or needed to get immediate money by means of a quickly written short story in a periodical); sudden weary descents into sentimentality; the tendency to drop into what has well been called coyness or archness at points at which his irony became too intricately complex even for him to handle. In a preface of 1912, written just after *Chance* had confirmed his decision to take an easier way (but he could not have gone on, in any case: he was cruelly compelled to live out his final years in a bitter mixture of the sort of over-honoured fame which his best works had always despised, and profound – and to ourselves, now, needless – regret of conscience) he famously wrote:

> Those who read me know my conviction that the world, the temporal world, rests on a few very simple ideas; so simple they must be as old as the hills. It rests notably on the idea of Fidelity.

That and similar 'official' statements, very 'British' in their resonance, have been employed to bolster up the popular notion of a greatly over-simplified Conrad, an Englishman – or 'assimilated Pole' – who was (he understandably liked to claim) "adopted by the genius of the English language". However, the vast majority of serious critics, to their credit, have not been taken in by any of this – even while few have denied Conrad the 'right' to have taken the course he did (Ford confessed, without a trace of malice, that he found the later work simply irrelevant). Carl Bennett, for example, citing that passage as the 'golden text' for the simplistic view, adds:

> But a statement of 1895, and allowed by Conrad in the preface to the definitive edition of *Almayer's Folly*, is much nearer to the scepticism and pessimism of his artistic vision, especially when taken in conjunction with the franker, grimmer tone of intimate correspondence...

> After speaking of the bonds that unite mankind, he adds that all men's hearts "must endure the loads of the gifts from heaven: the curse of facts and the blessings of illusions, the bitterness of our wisdom and deceptive consolation of our folly".

Of the important influences upon Conrad that have been traced, two stand out: those of Schopenhauer and Buddhism. But for all intents and purposes they are really one, since Schopenhauer himself also had turned to Buddhism as the most humanly uncongenial system he could find outside his own. The Schopenhauer influence is impossible to miss; the Buddhist, so far as we are dealing with Buddhism itself as distinct from the Schopenhauerean version, is perhaps best explored by means of comparison. Even more fruitful, especially in the light of letters to Graham written towards the end of the 1890s, is the comparison with gnosticism – also easily traceable in the work of Hardy, Kafka, Kipling and countless other major and minor writers.

To those who may feel that the presence of Ford in Conrad's life can be over-emphasized, it must be added that he himself had invited Ford to share the intimacy of his creative mind – a man cannot have a pilotfish in waters other than his own – and that therefore Ford always represented, for him, artistic conscience; not only did Ford possess this, but also he had the burden of Conrad's projected upon him. Of course the younger man learned rather more from the older, than vice versa – it would be foolish to try to deny it – and the clear narrative of *The Good Soldier* shows this; but Ford had a powerfully symbolic significance for Conrad which did not operate in reverse. Freud, in discussing his own relationship with his friend Fliess, spoke of an element of "unruly homosexuality", alluding not, of course, to physical attraction but rather to heterosexual erotic feelings displaced onto a man. The same element was present in Conrad's attitude towards Ford: when the older Violet Hunt 'took over', or appeared to take over, Ford, in 1908, he was jealous. But this element was not (I think) present in Ford's own attitude. However, the relationship between Conrad and Ford, of the greatest possible interest from points of view both literary and psychological, has yet to be written about fully, and with due sympathy for, and understanding of, both parties.

During the period following the publication of *An Outcast of the Islands* (1896) – a somewhat sentimental novel set in Malaya, featuring among others the Almayer of his first novel, more reminiscent of his final fiction than anticipatory of his best ("he writes so as to mask and dishonour his genius" Wells wrote – noting, too, its poor workmanship), and his marriage three weeks after this to Jessie George (who was, he said, "no trouble at all"), Conrad worked, at various times, on *The Nigger*, on an abortive fragment called *The Sisters* (published after his death), on various stories, and on *The Rescue* (first called "The Rescuer"). This novel tried to deal with his personal problems in a manipulative and wishfulfilling way, and he could not finish it; yet at the same time it represented to him the way of the potboiler towards which, with the ability he now knew he possessed, he was – naturally enough – always tempted. However, towards the end of his career, when he had no more to say, he revived it, finished it, published it, and added to its title a significantly defiant subtitle: "A Romance of the Shallows". The old irony was now working in reverse. When Pinker asked him what the Nobel Prize committee might look out for if they were to consider him, he suggested this novel. But *The Rescue* in that form is the nearest its author did come to a potboiler! He alluded, in a Note to it, to the "avarice which seeks its treasure in the hearts of men and women".

The Nigger of The "Narcissus"

The first story Conrad wrote which demonstrated that he was capable of a real masterpiece, though it is not quite one itself, was *The Nigger of The "Narcissus"*. This is the work in which he found his own voice, and began to resolve the conflict in himself between nihilism and responsibility, between the wildness and the terrors of the sea and the need to move over it, if not quite with an over-simplified 'Fidelity', then at least with some graceful mastery – some masterly grace.

Five questions about *The Nigger* deserve an answer. First, is it 'racist' (as it has been called by the conscientious editor of the Penguin edition)? Concomitantly, to what extent, if at all, is it a reflection of what has been described – again by the Penguin editor – as a 'reactionary' outlook? Thirdly, is the undoubtedly shifting identity of the narrative voice a result of authorial confusion, and is it therefore truly inconsistent and ambiguous – or does it work? Fourthly, how well does it work as an allegory (in its sense of 'an extended metaphor in which one thing is put in guise of another'), and what, if it does or tries to, is it allegorical of? Finally, to what extent is it autobiographical? How did Conrad transmogrify his own experiences in it? For he had sailed in a vessel called the *Narcissus*, and for just this once he did not change its name (it is the only case in all his fiction in which he did not change the name of a ship). The last matter may be disposed of first.

As he wrote *The Nigger* Conrad was, if only nominally, considering a return to the sea. We might say that his career as an author seemed to him to depend on the artistic success or failure of the book. Yet he had to sell it, too. We must appreciate how he felt about this predicament. Karl rightly states that the "very name of the ship... must have penetrated some area of experience... that lay beyond self-awareness, in those recesses that were already stirring and moving him towards his next and final career. The... name... apparently fitted into his view of art itself, as something based on mirrors, memories and reflections..." For him *The Nigger* was make-or-break, was the turning-point.

It was April 1884, and Conrad had just left the *Ravensdale* at Madras, upon which he had been serving as second mate, on account of a rift with its captain, whom he believed to be lacking in professionalism (he was: a few weeks later he stranded his ship and was relieved). Therefore, his own professionalism under fire, he was in a crisis of nerves special even to one of his temperament. He went from Madras to Bombay, and on 28 April signed on as second officer on the *Narcissus*, which he later described as a "lovely ship, with all the graces of a yacht". Towards the end of his life he told his French friend and biographer Jean-Aubry:

> Most of the personages I have portrayed actually belonged to the crew of the real *Narcissus*, including the admirable Singleton (whose real name was Sullivan) [Conrad's memory played him false: Sullivan was on another of his ships], Archie, Belfast and Donkin.

He gave Jean-Aubry more detail, with a fair but not absolute accuracy.

James Wait, the 'nigger', seems to have been based on more than one person: on a Joseph Barron whose death he described to Jean-Aubry, on another man, George White – and on other sailors, white as well as black. As he defensively remarked, "I do not write history, but fiction, and I am therefore entitled to choose as I please." Thus, although those critics, most notably Norman Sherry, who have traced the links between Conrad's experience and his fiction have performed sterling service, they have not established (as some believe) that he was an autobiographer rather than a novelist. What they have shown, instead, is how history can occasionally be transformed into art. We may be reminded of Aristotle (*Poetics*, 9):

> The difference between the historian and the poet is not that one writes in prose and the other in verse; Herodotus might be put into verse... The difference is that the one tells of what did happen and the other of the sorts of thing that could happen. Because of that poetry is a thing more philosophical and more worthy of serious attention than history: poetry concerns itself with universal truths, while history treats of sets of particular facts.

Prose fiction hardly existed in Aristotle's day, or not as we know it; and he could also have added (possibly he did, and it is unrecorded) that the poet (or novelist) could hardly infer such 'universal truths' as he was capable of establishing except from sets of histories of particular facts.

The hateful Donkin is not Conrad's representation – as he has woodenly been taken to be – of a socialist (his friend Graham was a socialist), but just an example of a man who is often found preaching anything (communism, fascism, end-of-the-worldism). Such a type cares for nothing in the least except his grievance. He has been taken by some as over-exaggerated, but it is hard to point to a more successful and dramatic a representation of such a type. Conrad learned here from Dickens; but he really did learn.

In certain respects *The Nigger* is nearer to a poem than to a novel or novella, both in its deliberately heightened language (sometimes this goes over the top) and in its fabulous qualities. It owes much, and not obliquely, to the most famous literary ballad ever written: Coleridge's "Rime of the Ancient Mariner". That influence persists, and becomes even more specific, in *The Shadow Line* of almost twenty years later.

Now to the matters of Conrad's alleged 'racism' and 'reactionary politics', as Watts misleadingly put it. The scrupulous editor of the Penguin edition of *The Nigger*, Professor Cedric Watts, felt so troubled by these that he felt bound to announce: "I think that the prestige of this vivid novel is now, partly for good reasons, in decline." But he then added that it had "outlived many judges" and "may well outlive more". As the book in which Conrad discovered, all on his own, a voice adequate to his majestic imaginative powers, one may feel confident that it will. It seems odd to consent to edit it for the popular market if it really does break the rules of political correctness.

Watts, as well as failing to understand that Conrad was actually challenging the role of the 'nigger' as the 'lowest of the low' stereotype, makes much of what he chooses to call Conrad's advocacy of 'hard primitivism', his 'attacks' on the highly emotional supporter of sailors' rights, the MP Samuel Plimsoll, and his use of the phrase "the repulsive mask of a nigger's soul" in his description of James Wait.

As, first, to "hard primitivism": this phrase was invented in 1935 in *Primitivism and Related Ideas in Antiquity*, edited by Arthur Lovejoy and others. Conrad had been a sailor who, in order to survive, had had to be tough: he could not in those days, in the storms and other troubles at sea which he encountered, have attended to the nice linguistic notions of Professor Watts or others fifty or more years later. So much for that. The mention of Plimsoll cannot be taken as critical – and he was in any case later praised by Conrad for ensuring better conditions at sea. Above all, one cannot purge the speech of an authors' characters because this might seem embarrassing in the context of a modern committee meeting. When Conrad read the socialist-anarchist Cunninghame Graham's ironic article "Bloody Niggers" in the Marxist periodical *The Social Democrat* he told him (just after finishing *The Nigger*): "very good, very telling". What, then, can Professor Watts think that the 'racist' and 'reactionary' Conrad, who could appreciate Graham's ironic "bloody niggers", had in mind in *The Nigger*?

The narrator, or one of them, stated of Wait:

> He held his head up in the glare of the lamp – a head vigorously modelled into deep shadows and shining lights – a head powerful and misshapen with a tormented and flattened face – a face pathetic and brutal: the tragic, the mysterious, the repulsive mask of a nigger's soul.

Watts comments: "the racism of this passage can be mitigated by noting it is the mask, rather than the soul, which is declared 'repulsive'; but the declaration remains irremediably racist".

Well, Conrad is dealing with the world of what Watts calls "common and casual prejudice", and, as a highly self-conscious artist, who wants to make people 'see', he has to be realistic about it. This is the world itself, rough and nasty and common and prejudiced. What, in such a context as a violent storm, could be a 'mitigation'? Watts is dictating, no less, and with a prissy zeal, that Conrad has no right even to depict such shocking verbal illiberalism. If it existed, then revise or re-arrange the facts – blot them out! Change the title! The facts of how nasty or misguided people actually talk and think, of the crew's survival, of Wait's death (how could a truly repulsive man's death be moving?), are in this book, not as some challenge to critics' speech-habits, but to Conrad's and to his common readers' own delicate and humane sensibilities. The mask of the nigger's soul is recorded as repulsive because to the crew, it seems so.

But, if it is well and firmly understood that *The Nigger* contains no 'racism' or 'reactionary politics', but rather the exact opposite, then it, may be conceded that Conrad might have chosen to be more delicate about how he expressed himself, had he not been desperately anxious to please W. E. Henley, in whose *New Review* it was to be serialized. Thus it may decently be argued that Conrad's strategy of presentation was very slightly misjudged: a word or phrase could have clarified what he meant. Conrad was well aware of Henley's wild imperialism, and privately criticized it. But he was nevertheless not reluctant to include the famous passage about the *Narcissus*: "A great ship!... The great flagship of the race; stronger than the storm! and anchored in the open sea." But so far as 'race' here does not mean just 'water' (Conrad possessed dictionaries), it means 'human race' and so to be a flagship of that race is not to be 'superior'. Probably, though, this passage was indeed a sly appeal to Henley's feelings. Yet there is no real imperialistic implication: the crew has survived a terrible storm, the ship is sailing into the Port of London, and this is how it would collectively express itself, were it articulate. But it is not one of Conrad's finest passages.

The Nigger, although realistic on the surface – even deliberately impressionistic, borrowing from Crane's *Red Badge of Courage* as it borrows from Maupassant's *Bel Ami* for some details of Wait's death – is above all poetic and allegorical. Where Conrad is immature in it is in his handling of the narrative line. The distinctions between the various voices have often been noticed. There are (at least): an 'I', an individual crewman, a 'we' the voice of the crew; an unidentified voice which refers to the crew as 'they'; and there is (possibly) another identified voice, an 'omniscient' author of some lyrical and analytical passages. It is not enough to argue with Ian Watt that Conrad "is at liberty to use his pretended narrator in whatever way will best serve his interests". Of course he is. But, alas, he occasionally uses him against his own interests: there is a confusion, and the function of each voice has not been fully worked out. Hence, almost immediately, in "Youth" and then in *Lord Jim*, the invention of Charlie Marlow as narrative device: the introduction of a definite point of view, not at all Conrad's own, but consistent. (Conrad is such a subtle writer that eventually his reader must explore the nature of the relationship between Conrad's point of view, for which his fiction – until he gives up – is in constant search, and the more clear-cut one which he invented for Marlow.)

But for some of the time the narrative of *The Nigger* does work. In particular, a valuable distinction may be made between an individual crewman's point of view, and the 'we' of the whole. Within a very few years, in France, Jules Romains, Georges Duhamel and others would invent 'unanimism', a method by which the crowd itself (of a block of flats, a district, a city, a country) would be given the 'voice' (a factitious thing, but one which these authors felt they could imaginatively capture – and gradually 'improve') which these interesting and idealistic theorists then felt it deserved. Zola had been working towards such a method, and so had many other novelists in many other countries. The unanimists had a somewhat rosy view of human nature (it was to be corrected by their war experiences), but Conrad did not. If his view was not really wholly pessimistic (had it been, he would not have written books at all) it was at the least realistic. The thin and reedy whine of the politically correct, that fine words butter parsnips, that history (and why, in due course, not texts themselves?) must be 'improved', artificially drained of its blood and terror, was not for him.

Had Conrad revised this text in later life when he had attained mastery (*The Nigger* announces a master, but its author is only on the verge of it) then he might have made fruitful changes, and separated the 'we' more clearly from the multiform 'I'. As it is, the lyrical passages may fairly be taken as the articulated view of the crew as a whole. 'We' are going to mutiny on behalf of James Wait; 'we' found him repulsive; 'we' refused to mutiny; 'we' acclaimed England; 'we' are not consistent. And what crowd is? It is the individuals who are variously merciful to, or betray, James Wait. Donkin abuses him and steals his money. Belfast gives him aid. Singleton is indifferent. That is how it would be, how it has been in 'real life', that always politically incorrect phenomenon. Conrad is preaching neither 'irrationalism' nor 'hard primitivism': he is preaching nothing at all. But a vitality is required to survive a terrible storm, and it is (rightly or wrongly) superstitious about its causes (is Coleridge politically incorrect in his approach to albatrosses?). The storm is the same one, as Conrad himself said, as that worked out at a more realistic level in *Typhoon*. Here it serves a more allegorical purpose for all the finely authentic description of it.

We are on a ship of fools here. Twice Conrad specifically refers to folly. Each character is a different sort of fool (or idiot, used in its original sense: private, uninitiated person). But the text underlying *The Nigger* is Coleridge's "Ancient Mariner". Wait's strangeness and his nearness to the possession of the secret of death (which he wants to deny) works both ways: Singleton (we shall encounter him again, as MacWhirr in *Typhoon*) and the boatswain both regard him as bad luck. His name suggests that he is a weight, a burden, and that he thus holds back the ship. The crew "commenced to believe Singleton, but with unshaken fidelity dissembled to Jimmy", "our Jimmy", the "tormentor of all our moments". "What makes mankind tragic is not that they [sic] are the victims of nature, but that they are conscious of it," Conrad wrote to Graham. And one thinks in that connection of the moving passage about the gallant ship's cat, Tom, who:

> came out from somewhere. He had an ovation. They snatched him from hand to hand, caressed him in a murmur of pet names. They wondered whether he had "weathered it out"; disputed about it. A squabbling argument began. Two men came in with a bucket of fresh water, and all crowded round it; but Tom, lean and mewing, came up with every hair astir and had the first drink.

This magnificent cat, Tom, is "not conscious of it" – but he had his problems, too, and he hid away mysteriously, as cats do – and is thus the unequivocal, ironic, untragic little thirsty hero. He is deferred to. And it as an account of storm and trial that *The Nigger* functions most naturally and perfectly. It is thus an imperfect masterpiece, in which Conrad has not yet reached the top of his narrative bent. "It is the book by which... as an artist striving for the utmost sincerity of expressing, I am willing to stand or fall" he wrote in a copy he gave to a friend. We all know that he stands.

III THE MAJOR WORKS (2)

The Inheritors

The Inheritors (1901), the political satire and roman à clef which Ford and Conrad eventually issued ahead of their work on Ford's "Seraphina" (which became *Romance*, 1903), is more interesting than critics have liked to take it to be. Its main thrust derives from both authors' hatred of (and despair about) Joe Chamberlain and 'his' (as it may justly be put, although others were involved) Boer War, which Conrad equated with the Belgian wickedness in the Congo which he had seen with his own eyes, and which had, for good measure, done for his good health. *The Inheritors* is not a major work (nor was it intended to be: it is light satire), but it helps to establish just how much Ford's presence inspired Conrad, gave more confidence and depth to his irony, and confirmed him in his more subversive convictions. Ford wrote the first draft of most of the book, but (although, as an honorary and fairly newly-fledged Englishman he was occasionally nervous to outsiders such as Garnett about it) Conrad welcomed it – indeed, it was he, Ford wrote, who gave each scene its "final tap". Written just after the completion of *Lord Jim,* it had been exhaustively discussed between the two authors, and so – like *Romance* – reflects the nature of the very first months of Conrad's intimacy with Ford. That he fully identified himself with the novel (despite some apparent disclaimers, made out of nervousness about his commitment to Ford) there can be no doubt. In one of the very few attempts at a serious consideration of it, by Frederick Karl, much of it is ascribed to Ford's 'misogyny'. It should be noted not only that this is a spectacular misreading, but also a prime example of how the best-willed professor, in his capacity as 'owner of literature', can selectively instruct us in what is to be termed irony and what is not. The irony here is certainly more Fordian than Conradian, and should therefore be discussed in the context of the former's work; but, alas, Conrad enjoyed it and profited from it.

Conrad and irony

Conrad's (not to speak of Ford's) use of irony is now an essential element in literary definitions of the term – it adds to its history. Conrad is perhaps an ironist above all – an ironist entirely foreign to the nicer world of his more 'honourable' and safely liberal friend Galsworthy. Galsworthy had never smuggled guns or tried to kill himself (and explained away the wound as the result of a duel with a sinister South American) – his worst offence to society had been to have been idle at Oxford! It is handling of irony that pulls Conrad fully clear, and far above, such novelists as Arnold Bennett and H.G. Wells, both superior to the decent Galsworthy ("a shade too little of a blackguard", as Walter Raleigh said of the poet laureate, Robert Bridges). Both were commercial men, but ones still very effectively haunted, and quite often enough, by authentically dark and depressed visions – the one by his canny psychological realism (seen in relatively isolated form in *The Card*), the other by the poetic savagery of his angry disbelief in his own scientistic utopianism (for example, *Mr Blettsworthy on Rampole Island*). Bennett even wrote, generously, of *The Secret Agent* that although it was the kind of thing he reckoned to handle himself, "I respectfully retire from the comparison". He was right, as his excursions into 'political material', not discreditable, clearly demonstrate. He did not quite have the courage of his ironic convictions. But such generosity is endearing – and Bennett is always worth reading on Conrad.

We must pause, with the pioneering Conrad mainly in mind, to give a brief consideration to the nature of irony, and take a look at some of the multitudinous levels – some of them shockingly 'innocent' – at which it can function. The stipends of professors drop regularly and plumply onto bountiful carpets, whereas Conrad with his taking up of mere authorship – abandoned even the rough, 'all-found' nature of a naval career for nothing much regular at all. The former thus tend to revise or rationalise – with 'moderation' in mind the irony of which his writing is so redolent, even to seem insensitive to its fury and to the subversive elements in it. The common reader, who cannot claim to own literature (if only by the dubious virtue of his too ignorant engagement with it), may therefore, if with only a strictly temporary legitimacy, beware a little: his reprehensibly imperfect vision of the man Conrad as he actually was, before he was slaughtered, cut up into demonstrative strips, dried, and exhibited in confirmation of a theory (never mind which, so long as it is a theory) has a sort of weakly nostalgic appeal. Irony is from the Greek 'to dissimulate', and there are many more ways of dissimulation than the simple "saying the opposite of what you think" (as the term is too frequently taken to mean). A relatively puerile ironic statement (which would be properly 'marked down' in the classroom) might, for example, be: "Twentieth-century professors have all been late nineteenth-century seamen and have instructionally referred to, what the crew called a nigger, as a *blackperson* or *Blackperson*, at the height of a life-threatening storm". Irony mockingly gives the impression of great restraint (or casual light-heartedness), a commodity highly valued by 'establishment persons' – the cruellest pronouncements are usually made, by these, unironically, and in a self-consciously 'moderate' manner (and are thus transformed into irony only in the jaundiced perception of certain dysgenic listeners). The ironist will even pretend that he is being funny when he is really being serious, and he will never admit to being ironic. But whether irony is intended (or even present) depends on the speaker. If a minister of government says, "if workers are given rights, then they will suffer", this is not ironic: he lives in a benign hope that his listeners will believe it. If a less responsible person, unburdened with affairs of state, and therefore able to be frivolously less unsophisticated, makes the same remark, then it might well be ironic: the speaker will imagine that he is pretending that he is a fool; he may, too, cringingly request 'correction' from "those who know and understand". Irony is, or can be, exceedingly subversive, and therefore often goes unrecognised by officials – or, by critics, exactly according to the timidity of their attitudes (this can be considerable: their appointments are by the grace of 'establishment people'). The revengeful chortle which can silently accompany it, however, may not always go unspotted (a streetwise millionaire can 'smell' an 'artist', even if he cannot understand him). It is sometimes only a matter of tone; in written material, it may frequently be inferred only from the general context. Job's "No doubt but ye are the people, and wisdom shall die with you" is probably the most famous of all pieces of undoubted irony, because it occurs in the Bible. It is rivalled only by Shakespeare's Mark Antony's praise of Brutus as an "honourable man". Good, recent criticism – influenced by Conrad's example himself allows, too, that irony may also be used as a term to describe a writer's "recognition of incongruities". in Conrad that takes the form of a kind of dark Polish gleefulness – a nihilistic gleefulness (such as we find in Hardy's "The Convergence of the Twain", about the Titanic disaster) that things are considerably less simple than they appear to be when they are presented by idealists, politicians or theorists. Polish history could itself be described as a bit 'ironic'. Irony is also a major element in humour. Conrad is not a straightforwardly comic writer, as both Dostoievski and Kafka (among other things) were; but he is a very funny one. Finally, irony, as a 'recognition of incongruities', can become – for men and women foolish or idealistic, or simply puzzled enough to find the public world an impossible place – a defensive way of life.

Lord Jim

Conrad was not as ironic in his first books as he became later. And Ford acted as catalyst for the full release of that famous irony. There is comparatively little of it in *Almayer's Folly, An Outcast of the Islands*, or even in *The Nigger* itself. *Lord Jim*, which at one level is an allegory or even parable of the artist's (Conrad's in particular) predicament, is almost without it. *Lord Jim* was written when we know that Conrad was working intermittently and often quarrelling and then making up to Ford. Both their wives were annoyed and felt that the other wife's husband was wasting her partner's time. Jessie much later admitted that Conrad needed "an equal", but at the time she was jealous both of Conrad's easy intimacy (they would laugh at things of which she had no inkling and did not think were funny) and of Elsie Ford, whom she rightly suspected of being more 'literary'. Yet *Lord Jim* – which has been called (dubiously, by theory-driven critics anxious to neutralize its power to disturb?) a "psychomoral novel", a "new fictional form evolving midway between Melville's *Benito Cereno* and Faulkner's *Absalom, Absalom!*", was very much Conrad's 'own thing' – something with which he had to get through specifically, to clear the ground, without Ford. A brief summary of *Jim's* plot is sufficient to demonstrate that Jim himself, its anti-hero and then hero, "the last protagonist in modern fiction who dies to redeem his honour", represents Conrad's notion of himself as artist, as what an artist ought to do and be. But 'artist' stands, of course, for 'man of conscience', 'ideal common reader' (every writer needs to be this) – for the person who sees things as they are and then goes on from there to make the journey into himself. Jim is chief mate on the steamship *Patna*. Conrad was 'romantically' and emotionally drawn to sail, so that we may see, even in that, an image of the (for him) uncongenial nature of the literary market. As Jim's story begins, the *Patna* is full of pilgrims bound for Mecca. Jim thinks that he has learned the way of the honourable sailor. But he is overtaken by the sort of event that overtakes all such over-confident men. The ship – which has no lifeboats – looks as though it is about to sink: he sees some crewmen lowering a boat in order to make their own escape. He thinks that he is 'all right', that he is just an onlooker who knows better. But his impulses betray all that idealism: he jumps into it (a representation of Conrad's impulse to employ his literary gifts, not to obtain a sufficiency, but for commercial purposes – the purposes of the Belgian exploitation of the Congo): what he jumps into is an "everlasting deep hole" – and yet, also, in his conduct "there was not the thickness of a sheet of paper between the right and wrong of his affair", which is an internal one. At this point, there is irony, but it is irony of events, not (yet) that of utterance. Thus the device of Marlow, as narrator, was invented partly in order to provide irony. Jim has a conscience: he needs to confess what he decided to call the cowardice which overtook him as he was watching the small crew jumping into the boat. Contrary to his belief, the *Patna* did not sink, but was salvaged by a French gunboat. But at a Court of Inquiry he has elected to face the consequences of *his* action. He is observed by Marlow – publicly stripped of his master's certificate. So now we see him, aided by Marlow, holding a series of positions ashore, all the time trapped under the eye of 'talkers', those who make, for themselves, a casual joy of his disgrace – a disgrace that is far more deeply acknowledged by him than they could even understand, and is *his*. Only his mentor Marlow can perceive this. He obtains a place as agent at a remote island trading-post, Patusan, in which he excels as a skilful, daring and practical man. Paradoxically, it has been his experience of an opposite to these qualities – chiefly, the cowardice and dishonourable sense of self-preservation which he so horribly discovered in himself just as he was feeling at his most complacent – which has enabled him to achieve them. To the aged chief Doramin he is "Tuan Jim", Lord Jim. To all he is possessed of "invincible supernatural power". In Kurtz of *Heart of Darkness* we saw such prestige misused; here we saw it well used and honoured.

Then "the famous Gentleman Brown", "supposed to be the son of a baronet", "the show ruffian on the Australian coast" (Conrad had met such men, which was perhaps why, later, as a socially acceptable writer, he tended to eschew their smoother counterparts, officers of government), a criminal adventurer, arrives with his band of thieves – "Rot his superior soul!" he remarks of Jim as he dies. Having stolen a schooner, Brown and his gang are in trouble: they need to reach Patusan in order to get provisions, and perhaps some "real ringing coined money!" Jim promises that he will rid the island of them without bloodshed. But he is betrayed. Doramin's son is killed. Jim therefore pays voluntarily with his life: he allows the angry and grieving Doramin to shoot him. He has failed, but he has atoned: " ...he understood. He had retreated from one world, for a small matter of an impulsive jump, and now the other, the work of his own hands, had fallen in ruins on his head... The dark powers would not rob him twice of his peace".

In *Jim* Conrad was, simultaneously, creating a parable of the artist as absurd perfectionist, dealing with his personal problems, and trying to write a romantic adventure acceptable to *Blackwood's*, in which it first appeared in serial form. *Youth*, in which he invented Marlow ("I think that is how he spelt his name"), also appeared in *Blackwood's*; it can be even be asserted that he was handed this device of a person narrator – on a silver platter – by the established practice of the regular writers for that magazine. So inextricably mixed were – and are – the paths of integrity and the market.

Heart of Darkness

Heart of Darkness was written immediately before *Jim*, which had originally been intended as a tale to complete the three-story volume *Youth*. In *Youth* (its epigraph from Grimm reads: "... but the dwarf answered: 'No, something human is dearer to me than the wealth of the world' ") we see Marlow established; and there we learn more about him than we shall really learn again, he being in the late novels only a device. We understand from *Youth* what kind of writer Conrad (his two prentice novels out of the way, the direction of his path at last hacked out in *The Nigger*) wants now to be: one who will plough his way through impossibilities, who will somehow try to revolutionise the nature of the popular market while knowing that he cannot. The sea is Conrad's first and foremost metaphor, and we hear Marlow tell the story of his own initiation into manhood, and get sentimentally drunk at the end of it:

> "Ah! The good old time – the good old time. Youth and the sea. Glamour and the sea! The good, strong sea, the salt, bitter sea, that could whisper to you and roar at you and knock your breath out of you". He drank again.

In *Heart of Darkness* it is goodbye to illusion, though *Youth* ends:

> And we all nodded at him: the man of finance, the man of accounts, the man of law, we all nodded at him over the polished table that like a still sheet of brown water reflected our faces, lined, wrinkled; our faces marked by toil, deceptions, by success, by love; our weary eyes looking still, looking sideways, looking always, looking anxiously for something out of life, that while it is expected is already gone – has passed unseen, in a sigh, in a flash – together with the youth, with the strength, with the romance of illusions.

Thus established, Marlow tells part of a very different story in *Heart of Darkness*, which was 'obviously', Conrad wrote in his Note to *Youth*, "written in another mood": "anybody can see that it is anything but the mood of wistful regret, of reminiscent tenderness".

It is a mood of furious indignation, the same kind of mood in which so many of Dickens's novels (especially *Hard Times*) were written. It is so 'awful' a story (and sometimes Conrad's language does fail in just that way) that it could not be told directly, as by some 'omniscient narrator'. The journey it describes is one to the 'reader's own moral core'. It is a simple enough story in itself. Conrad's English recollection of his African experience of 1890 lay at the heart of this darkness, and so Marlow tells the tale to four companions, on a ship in the Thames estuary, while they are waiting for the tide to turn (for history to change its appalling nature)? He says at one point: "All Europe contributed to the making of Kurtz".

Marlow was sent to Africa to replace a river-steamer captain who had been murdered in a scuffle with natives (over two black hens). The Company men he meets are interested only in one thing: the ivory they can extract from the interior. In one sense, in their blandness and their blindness to all decency and justice, they are 'worse' than the demonic Kurtz, who does 'know'. They are oblivious to the terrible sufferings endured by the natives. Robert Kimbrough puts it as well as it has ever been put in his 1984 World Classics edition of *Youth*:

> All of Europe... contributed to the making of Kurtz – Europe: safe, civilized, scheduled, masculine, literate, Christian, and dead. Kurtz, a European 'Knight', sets out on a crusade to win the hearts and minds of a lesser people, ignorant of the degree to which Africa is dangerous, wild, timeless, feminine, unfettered by letters, religious, and vibrant. His love turns to rape when he discovers how unfitted he is to master the magnificent vitality of a natural world. The difference between Europe and Africa is the difference between two secondary symbols: the European woman who has helped puff up Kurtz's pride and the African woman who has helped to deflate him.

The ivory (this is of course widely supposed to have aphrodisiac qualities) represents both money and treasure. It should thus be noted that, as in many of Conrad's earlier books, there is here a pun on the word, or notion of, 'treasure': it functions both as real treasure, and as cash, money power, 'creation of wealth'. Here the ivory is corrupted by greed. In Nostromo the "silver of the mine" is similarly tainted. And in each case the male sexual corruption is made explicit – in *Heart* the sexual theme is perhaps a little blurred, or more generalised; but in *Nostromo* Gould's deliberate choice to rape his wife's wisdom and beauty – in the interests of greed – is made perfectly clear. In *Lord Jim* the theme is merely adumbrated, but it is there.

Marlow's interest is aroused by a man called Kurtz, a super-agent reputed to be the most adept of all at obtaining ivory (he is at one point described as being made of ivory), cultivated (he is a painter), and idealistic. Hearing that Kurtz is seriously ill, Marlow makes an expedition to 'rescue' him; he believes that he is in search of a model of Western, political altruism. He discovers a male who exactly symbolises what Western 'politics' would be were it to become self-aware – for Kurtz is, at the least, horrifyingly self-aware. But Kurtz's function as a 'human being' is also what Western politics actually is: Conrad caricatures this as Belgian greed in the Congo, something which after all Conrad had himself seen and suffered from.

He is a man who collects human heads. They decorate the poles outside his hut. He has become (as Tuan Jim will so differently be) a god to the natives.

Men and women were able to read about Kurtz in 1898-9 in *Blackwood's*, and then in 1902 in the volume *Youth*. They were able, thirty or so years later, actually to witness him – as "the cultivated Nazi", as (to take a famous example) an Ernst Jünger – actually himself a very noted and capable 'symbolic novelist' who liked to dine in wartime Paris with 'civilised' Frenchmen and who 'deplored' the war. One wonders if Jünger – a highly intelligent, icy, loveless, factitious monster who had composed a book (*Auf den Marmorklippen*, 1939, *On the Marble Cliffs*) ambiguously 'critical' of the Nazis, and had seen it eventually suppressed – ever read *Heart of Darkness*, and what he thought of Kurtz. For the tale is prophetic, too. Jünger himself had once tried to help create a Nazi-like party much more 'refined' than the Nazis themselves were. This Kurtz still lives: one century old.

Marlow's journey into the heart of darkness is the nearest Conrad ever came to poetry; it could be written as poetry (a form which must elude a Pole writing in English, late learned); indeed, it needs to be thus transformed; it is not quite 'right' in prose – in that way he did almost overreach himself:

> Kurtz discoursed. A voice! a voice! It rang deep to the very
> last. It survived his strength to hide in the magnificent folds of
> eloquence the barren darkness of his heart. Oh, he struggled!
> he struggled! [just as his creator struggles with language here.]
> The wastes of his weary brain were haunted by shadowy images
> now – images of wealth and fame revolving obsequiously round
> his unextinguishable gift of noble and lofty expression. My

intended, my station, my career, my ideas – these were the subjects for the occasional utterances of elevated sentiments. The shade of the original Kurtz frequented the bedside of the hollow sham, whose fate it was to be buried presently in the mound of primeval earth. But both the diabolic love and the unearthly hate of the mysteries it had penetrated fought for the possession of that soul satiated with primitive emotions, avid of lying fame, of sham distinction, of all the appearances of success and power.

Then, shortly, follow the most famous (and bitterly unheeded) words Conrad ever wrote:

He cried out in a whisper of some image, at some vision – he cried out twice, a cry that was no more than a breath

"The horror! The horror!"

It is magnificent; Conrad is almost able to tell us, in the context, what this "horror" is, this sense of deep rottenness which is experienced at the very point of possession of a hitherto lost paradise, as Marlow continues:

I remained to dream the nightmare out to the end, and to show my loyalty to Kurtz once more. Destiny. My destiny! Droll thing life is – that mysterious arrangement of merciless logic for a futile purpose. The most you can hope from it is some knowledge of yourself that comes too late – a crop of unextinguishable regrets. I have wrestled with death. It is the most unexciting contest you can imagine... I affirm that Kurtz was a remarkable man. He had something to say. He said it. Since I had peeped over the edge myself, I understood better the meaning of his stare, that could not see the flame of the candle, but was wide enough to embrace the whole universe, piercing enough to penetrate all the hearts that beat in the darkness. He had summed up – he had judged. "The horror!"...

This is, then, "magnificent", but will not yet quite do – it is flawed ultimately, by the very kind of rhetoric that the use of the word "magnificent" itself suggests. The language itself cannot quite carry the enormous poetic weight of its own implications. Conrad is now being held up by his not being able to be a poet, by his own choice of a foreign language in which to express himself. Perhaps had he remained in Poland, suffered his fate as Pole, he might have been able to be a poet, and one better than his father had been. But then his subject would have been that of remaining in Poland, or at least of returning to Poland to become a Pole again...

He chose thus, in part, because to say (like Kurtz) what he had to say, to declare his knowledge of the darkness in himself, and in everybody else, in a language actually native to him, one closely familiar, a medium he could think in without thinking – would have been just too much, too overwhelmingly 'horrible'. His wild language in his letters to his uncomprehending, philistine agent Pinker, were full of desperate phrases about 'survival'.

What he now needed was something a little cooler, something which would enable him to survive the intensity of his searing self-awareness: this need would be fulfilled by the discovery of more irony, the finding of a capacity to write in an ironic, non-rhetorical style, a style not clumsily imitative of poetry, one which, with Ford's help, he could learn (as William Empson later phrased it in a famous poem) from a despair.

IV THE MAJOR WORKS (3)

Typhoon

Conrad finished *Typhoon* in January 1901. After serialisation that year in the *Pall Mall Gazette*, it appeared, with "Amy Foster", "To-Morrow" and "Falk", as *Typhoon* in 1902. He later told his friend Richard Curle that it had been "meant as a pendant to the storm in *The Nigger*, the ship in this case being a steamship". It is based on an anecdote Conrad heard, and on a captain named John MacWhirr under whom he had once sailed – on the *Highland Forest* in 1887. But it is nearer to pure invention – though of course he had sailed through many storms – than most of his works. As a story (it is just over 30,000 words), it has been consistently underrated, perhaps because it is atypical: a straightforward story, simply told, and without trimmings. It is an account of a steamship's survival of a fearful storm; but the real story is of the extraordinarily ordinary captain, MacWhirr, who muddles through triumphantly. The chief interest of the story, apart from the description of the storm, lies in the characterisation of MacWhirr, which is in fact – though it has been largely missed – a remarkable tour de force. It is here that we encounter for the first time the influence of Ford. More precisely, however, we should say: the influence of the joint state of mind which the two men achieved, as a result of some almost miraculous symbiosis of character. Ford has been much berated for stating that he "taught Conrad to write". He didn't (of course); but he alone brought out, in Conrad, what he needed to write: *Nostromo* and *The Secret Agent*. The first sight we get of this is in the characterisation of that amazing man MacWhirr. MacWhirr is certainly Conrad's own, there is no doubt about that. But one cannot imagine either his being able to create him in the absence of Ford – or his having sat down to write *Typhoon* without talking MacWhirr gleefully over with his friend. He had learned the tone of the opening characterisation from Ford's conversation. It cannot be conceived of without considering Ford; and it is a very fine piece of writing, one of which, curiously enough (or perhaps it is not so curious), Ford himself, alone, would not become capable of writing until many years later, when he came to write his masterpieces. Few similar passages of English prose combine genuinely amazed humane respect with kindly irony in so incisive a manner:

> Captain MacWhirr of the steamer *Nan-Shan* had a physi-
> ognomy that, in the order of material appearances, was the

exact counterpart of his mind: it presented no marked characteristics of firmness or stupidity; it had no pronounced characteristics whatever; it was simply ordinary, irresponsive, and unruffled.

The only thing his aspect might have been said to suggest, at times, was bashfulness; because he would sit, in business offices ashore, sunburnt and smiling faintly, with downcast eyes. When he raised them, they were perceived to be direct in their glance and of blue colour. His hair was fair and extremely fine, clasping from temple to temple the bald dome of his skull in a clamp as of fluffy silk. The hair of his face, on the contrary, carroty and flaming, resembled a growth of copper wire clipped short to the line of the lip; while, no matter how close he shaved, fiery metallic gleams passed, when he moved his head, over the surface of his cheeks. He was rather below the medium height, a bit round-shouldered, and so sturdy of limb that his clothes always looked a shade too tight for his arms and legs. As if unable to grasp what is due to the difference of latitudes, he wore a brown bowler hat, a complete suit of brownish hue, and clumsy black boots. These harbour togs gave to his thick figure an air of stiff and uncouth smartness. A thin silver watchchain looped his waistcoat, and he never left his ship for the shore without clutching in his powerful, hairy fist an elegant umbrella of the very best quality, but generally unrolled... Having just enough imagination to carry him through each successive day, but no more, he was tranquilly sure of himself; and from the very same cause he was not in the least conceited... It was impossible in Captain MacWhirr's case... to understand what under heaven could have induced that perfectly satisfactory son of a petty grocer in Belfast to run away to sea. And yet he had done that very thing at the age of fifteen... His father never really forgave him for this undutiful stupidity. "We could have got on without him," he used to say later on, "but there's the business. And he an only son, too!" His mother wept very much after his disappearance. As it had never occurred to him to leave word behind, he was mourned over for dead till, after eight months, his first letter arrived from Talcahuano. It was short, and contained the statement: "We had very fine weather on our passage out."

MacWhirr really is an astonishingly unimaginative man. Too unimaginative, really, to be a hero, a character with whom the reader may identify. He appears comically, at first, even to Jukes, the chief mate, that deliberately commonplacely named grand hero. And yet MacWhirr is – this is just it – a real hero, and not one of romantic books. He embodies many paradoxes: as Conrad puts it, the "uninteresting lives of men so entirely given to the actuality of bare existence have their mysterious side". The sort of irony Conrad achieved in his description of MacWhirr, the perfection of which he owed to his friendship with Ford, may very well (and illustratively) be termed "recognition of incongruities".

So the end of it is that MacWhirr muddles through, or perhaps even just gets through without even exactly muddling. Jukes can write: "The skipper remarked to me the other day, 'There are things you find nothing about in books'. I think that he got out of it very well for such a stupid man." This at one level echoes what Conrad told Graham about the reason mankind is tragic: "What makes mankind tragic is not that they are victims of nature, but that they are conscious of it." MacWhirr is not "tragic": he is fortunate, "ignorant of life to the last", "disdained by destiny or by the sea". Yet he is so strange that he is 'natural'. *Typhoon* is Conrad the writer's tribute to the tough virtues of the unartistic world which his own creative imagination so painfully transmutes: the world which gives him strength and courage to exercise that terrible 'consciousness' of the 'tragedy' of existence. Marry this to one of the most vivid and beautiful images in *Nostromo* – that monumental book which fails only on the scale upon which all lives fail – the "paradise of snakes", and we have something of the complexity of the writer at his peak.

Nostromo

"The greatest novel of the twentieth century," wrote Walter Allen of *Nostromo*, and, whether we enjoy it or not, we cannot but grant the validity of the claim. It is, as Carl Bennett has claimed, "a prodigy of achievement which by reason of its scope of vision and its many-textured substance invites comparison with *War and Peace*". That scope of vision includes many strands of Western thinking, amongst the more obvious of which are Homer, Dante, Darwinism (or "transformism", known in ancient China), Junghanism – and, on the negative side, imperialism and the "social-Darwinist' or 'evolutionist' thinking of Herbert Spencer. Imperialism just now is officially looked upon to be a dead duck, which it was not at the turn of the century. *Nostromo*, though, is nevertheless up to date. Imperialism, since it is profitable, continues under other guises: in such notions as 'aid', 'European unity' and other fine phrases. Conrad's intention, and he was now functioning at his peak, was "to render the spirit of an epoch in the history of South America". He therefore invents a whole country, Costaguana (which can be rendered as 'shitcoast', although 'Costa', at a more innocent level, derives from the 'Costa' of Costa Rica, and guano, an important trade item, is 'manure'). Costaguana is, in an imaginative sense, Poland – and there is no country more suitable than Poland to illustrate the nature of modern politics. At the "centre of tragic awareness" Conrad puts a woman, Emily Gould, perhaps the most beautiful and profound of all his creations. Her chief oppressor is her husband, Charles Gould; a more subtle and modified portrait of Kurtz, Gould appears simply to be a decent modern businessman. In fact, because he could have been an enlightened man and also because he could have drawn upon his wife's wisdom, his capitulation to "materialistic interests" is positively Faustian.

Conrad initially planned *Nostromo* as a short novel; but it grew on him, possessed him, and ultimately threatened his peace of mind. Its end is spoiled because he could not continue with it; but this does not vitiate its visionary power. The essence of *Nostromo* is that there can be no reconciliation. In that sense it is probably the most pessimistic novel ever written. Flaubert, another who saw straight into the heart of the rottenness of modern political arrangements, was always Conrad's supreme master, was always "the divine presence". But Conrad could never have reached the heights of affirmation achieved by Flaubert in *Un Coeur Simple*. D.H. Lawrence, who admired Conrad, could never forgive him "for being so sad and for giving in". But Conrad dug deeper into himself than Lawrence ever could; since the latter, whenever he confronted himself, had to turn away. In common with many other writers of his calibre, a part of Conrad, the one which liked comfort and ease, deeply resented the writer's obsession with integrity and truth-telling – the tendency to be dissatisfied with 'incongruities'. During the whole of the time he was writing *Nostromo* he was in severe money trouble, and was having to turn out what he thought of as inferior work for money. He wrote to his agent Pinker of existence as "hell". *Nostromo* is about nothing if it is not about 'material interests'. Conrad was living out, within himself, all the many emotional dramas he depicts in the novel, but sustained by Ford, keeping himself just short of complete collapse. His egocentricity never brought him the least happiness; it is sadly instructive that it none the less seems to have been necessary to his genius.

Conrad and Ford's *Romance* was a partly botched rehearsal for Conrad's *Nostromo*, which is doubtless why Conrad allowed Ford to write some of the latter. So Ford was the paramount influence here. However, there were discussions with Graham, who had some (wholly external) characteristics in common with Charles Gould, such as that he had met his wife in Europe, and that he had red hair. Conrad liked Graham, and there is no doubt that he intended to make Gould into a lily that had festered rather than a mere weed. Viola, the Garibaldian, is based on Garibaldi himself. The detail of the dying Hirsch's final spitting into the face of Sotillo is taken from Garibaldi's autobiography. For Nostromo himself Conrad drew partly on the tale of a villainous sailor who had been entrusted with some silver, but more particularly on the character of the Corsican, Dominic Cervoni, whom he had known in his days as a gambler and adventurer. The name of Decoud comes from R.F. Burton's *Letters from the Battle-fields of Paraguay*: he is D. Juan Decoud, editor of *El Liberal*. But there is a close resemblance, too, between Decoud and the young Conrad himself at the time of his para-suicide: the portrait may be seen as a verdict on a past self.

Conrad also drew on Edward B. Eastwick's *Venezuela*, M. H. Harvey's *Dark Days in Chile* and G.F. Masterman's *Seven Eventful Years in Paraguay*. The last-named suffered torture very similar to that endured by Monygham, even to the extent of confessing to crimes of which he was guiltless.

But the main 'source' of *Nostromo* is itself fictional: the 'impartial' and 'eloquent' *History of Fifty Years of Misrule*, written, Conrad claims in his 'Note', by "my venerated friend, the late Don Jos Avellanos, Minister to the Courts of England and Spain etc, etc..." Professor Karl claims that this device is 'Borgean'; but Borges was passing through his third and fourth years while *Nostromo* was in the making... it is indeed a very 'modern' book for its time, 1904 – for books even more 'modern', one has to go right back, to Homer, Dante, Rabelais, Cervantes, Grimmelshausen. Latin American politics seem hardly to have changed at all. Conrad did brilliantly well to capture their brutal and tragic essence. To find parallels one has to turn to such much later novels as Miguel Asturias's *Señor Presidente* or Augusto Roa Bastos's *Yo el Supremo*; but one feels that these and other such Spanish-American writers had gratefully absorbed Conrad. Conrad never advocated revolution – but there is a sense in which he made himself a part of it, if an unwilling one, by always (by implication) deprecating oppression and corruption, not as an injustice collector (of one of those, he has given us a memorable portrait in Donkin) but as one who sees that these are violations of the spirit, of the real meaning of 'silver'.

The silver and the mine which hold it stand, in *Nostromo*, not only for money, the power it confers, and treasure – but also for luck, fortune, incorruptibility, integrity, and the unconsciousness of each individual. Ironically, too, they stand for conscience. One of the indubitable successes of the book is the manner in which this symbol coheres, is made to work at each of many levels. Reading the book is a profound mental experience, and no-one who reads it properly is ever quite the same again.

We see in the case of each character that what should have been good, self-enlightening, useful, helpful, is turned to corruption or defeat, and if not to that, then to devastation. Greed or lust for power seem inevitably to turn virtue, the truly precious, into vice; in the case of Gould ('gold'), the damned character of the novel just as his wife Emily and the wrecked, crippled, frustrated Monygham ("in a jam about money") are the 'saved', it serves as his continuous justification for his gradual moral decay. He is exactly what his wife is not: talker, briber, taker, corrupted humanitarian, perpetrator of lying clichés, apostle of material interests, the man who, finally, can be nothing, empty, without his cash and his possessions. If this was Conrad's means of putting the usurers and cash-men (upon whose grasping generosity he had to rely for a roof and warmth for his wife and family) into hell, then revenge had certainly been sublimated by the time he sat down – the pen often slipping from his gouty fingers – to write.

The continuing deterioration of Gould, the subtly depicted rejecter of the feminine, is one of the aspects of *Nostromo* that has not had full attention from critics, who tend to view the character as unfortunate, half-wise, only partially corrupt, or even as virtuous. Despite his fine talk, Gould is the maladministrator of the silver, and the evil genius of the book. The dictators and criminal politicians such as Sotillo are simply the products of a society deliberately kept in a state of lawlessness. Gould, who has been 'civilised' (educated at an English public school), ought to know better. But, although he is a capitalist, and representative of all that capitalism implies, especially of the greed that lies at its virtuous heart, the "haters of capitalists", such as the photographer who haunts Nostromo's death-bed, come off no better. Conrad does not see revolution as a humanising or reconciling force any more than Flaubert did. But those who see Conrad as a 'right-wing thinker' because of that should think again: he desired to see many of the things which revolution is supposed to bring about: freedom of thought and language; the right to be 'naturally local'; justice; the end of all kinds of economic exploitation of one large set of people by another smaller group ('the fittest' in the false social-Darwinist sense); and much else. It was just that he saw very clearly, and from personal experience, how revolutions do not have those results. However, Conrad has also, by critics who discern this, been claimed as a Marxist (rather in the same manner as the overrated Hungarian critic Lúkacs so famously and influentially "captured Balzac for Marxism"). But – although he would have approved of many of Marx's insights into the nature of capitalist society – he was not this, either: he was, just as Flaubert was, a disillusioned humane liberal who put imagination (which he made the 'business' to which he wished to 'attend') above a too cerebral and in any case futile political philosophy.

Ironically, tragically and paradoxically, the silver, the precious and beautiful metal, either corrupts or defeats each character in a different manner: each character is defined by his or her attitude to it. The regular politicos are, as usual, at the lowest level; the silver, to them, is simply a means of economic and therefore political control. Equally low is the grandiose business gangster, the North American Holroyd, for whom the silver mine provides a means of running, not a 'board', but a man (Gould) and of creating a Protestant empire (Sulaco). Emily Gould alone sees through Holroyd, who thinks of Sulaco only for a very small proportion of his grand time.

Charles Gould's father is driven to despair and an ignominious death by the manner in which the corrupt Costaguana government uses the San Tomé mine against him. Forced to lend money to a succession of governments, he is at last 'repaid' with the apparently useless silver mine – and required to pay in advance a five-year royalty on the "estimated yield". The trick reads like a list of 'traps to avoid' in an instruction manual to budding modern city magnates. He tells his son, at school in England, that he must never come back to Costaguana, that the "Gould concession" is a curse. But young Charles insists upon studying mining: his desire to exploit 'his' mine is greater than his love for Emily, even before he ever sees Sulaco. He must succeed at all costs, and thus prepares himself for further corruption: when Conrad causes him to say to Emily that "The best of my feelings are in your keeping", he is well aware of the irony. Gould's progressively corrupted feelings, his justificatory lies, have to be the substitutes for the children Emily might otherwise have had. "I pin my faith to material interests," he tells her, and he pretends to believe that all sorts of good things – "law, good faith, order, security" – will spring from these "material interests".

Gould's piety in this respect, together with his murder of his wife's vitality, is what makes him the most repulsive character in the book. Even the cowardly Hirsch is allowed his last spit. Sotillo is simply paradigmatic of Latin American brutality – he might easily be a sketch for a portrait of any latter-day dictator. Gould is early shown, in a subtle passage, to have the sadistic impulse of dictators in his breast. The "breathing image" of his father, now dead, is said to be no longer in Gould's 'power':

> This consideration, closely affecting his own identity, filled his breast with a mournful and angry desire for action... Only in the conduct of our action can we find the sense of mastery over the Fates. For his action, the mine was obviously the only field.

As Paul Kirschner explains in *Conrad: The Psychologist as Artist*, "Gould's identity has been built up on his psychic antagonism to his father, concretised in the... mine. Dying, Mr Gould upset the equilibrium of his son's personality." (One has only to think of Conrad's own father, the tormented rebel patriot and writer.) Once the 'equilibrium' of this young man is thus 'upset', he ceases to look 'at all' at the woman he believes he loves – and so he comes to blight her life. We are certainly supposed to note, however, chilling it may be for our own enterprises, the difference between Emily's and Charles's view of the mine: for both it is ostensibly a means of helping an oppressed people, but for him this 'help' very soon becomes, if it was not always, a justification formula; for her it is a real opportunity missed. Gould, like Nostromo, betrays his innate virtue, the silver in the mine. But Gould acts in a familiar Western pattern: that of imposing 'idea' on what appears to him to be chaos: although especially privileged, in the sense that an intuitive beauty is immediately present to him, in the person of his wife, he allows greed to take precedence over her, by over-simplifying a dangerous richness into a 'chaos' – we cannot, he pretends, have 'good things' without, in a hypocritical phrase now all to familiar to modern ears, 'creating wealth'. It is in his exposure of Western 'idealism' (the quest for the only conceivable 'afterlife' has become one in which we can continue to enjoy possession of our money) that Conrad is at his most ironic; perhaps only a Pole could have summoned up the necessary indignation. He was one of a few people of his time who saw, as Ford did, that the very meaning of 'wealth' could only ever be defined by the exercise and practice of a primary good will. His Gould is therefore not a man who might make use of statistical information in order to benefit individuals, but rather one who believed in them as 'an explanation of society', and is therefore a liar with them.

One of the key passages occurs in Chapter 6 of the section called "The

Isabels". Gould 'King of Sulaco', has decided on the course of action he must take to avert the threat to the mine. Emily looks at his face: "all sign of sympathy or any other feeling had disappeared". She looks at the watercolour sketch of the San Tomé mine she had made before Gould started to rework it: "Ah, if we had left it alone, Charley!" she exclaims. She says that they have disturbed a "good many snakes in that Paradise". He replies: "It is no longer a Paradise of snakes. We have brought mankind into it, and we cannot turn our backs upon them to go and begin a new life elsewhere." She pretends not to be afraid of his sudden retreat into the purely masculine malevolence of his "Policy", returning his "concentrated gaze" with a "brave assumption of fearlessness"; and she is beautifully described by Conrad as having the "vividness of a figure seen in the clear patches of sun that chequer the gloom of open glades in woods": that is, a natural creature, inhabiting, without taint, just such a "Paradise of snakes" as she herself painted in the past when the mine remained closed, and Gould was "unfallen". The implication of the phrase "Paradise of snakes" is that it is the human, even that it is Adam's interpretation of the 'knowledge' imparted by the snake (the messenger of evil, according to patriarchal religionists, to Eve) that is wrong, not the knowledge itself. But that theme is never worked out in Conrad's fiction, because he could not become the poet, in the English language, that he needed to be to attempt it. But there has not been an English-language poet quite up to this in the twentieth century, and so we have had to go to the Peruvian Vallejo, the Spaniard Lorca, and others to find men who either (Vallejo) truly deplored the wilful nature of their maleness, or (Lorca) who deliberately indulged their femininity, who "made it tremble", in the form of a neurasthenic (and, in the peculiarly *macho* Spanish circumstances, heroic) homosexuality. But at least in the character of Mrs Gould, Conrad was able to imply that the nature of human error lies in a masculine attempt to interpret 'knowledge' as an unnatural (and impossible) 'pure maleness', a heartlessly surgical attempt to remove the feminine element altogether, and to consign it to a 'weaker' – but not a different – gender, a gender therefore deformed by its being turned into a sort of 'soft parody' of the male, so that 'wo-*men*" (the *wo* meaning simply *wife*, i.e. 'of a man') may be judged, and evaded, as unmysterious, manipulated males. What we hardly find, though, in his novels, is psychological exploration of why this should be so – of why, for example, the most famous book about suffering every written, *Job* (the most textually corrupt book in the Bible), should be about *male* suffering. Thus we get little more than hints about the domestic arrangements of Charles and Emily

Gould. It was for him, with his sexual demands on his 'stupid' Jessie (who was, we have to remember, "no trouble at all"), a little too near the bone. But Conrad would have understood, had it been pointed out to him, how unseemly, and flagrantly scandalous, this aspect of the theme of *Job* is.

The "paradise of snakes" passage reveals a hatred, almost a rejection, of technology and commerce which the majority of Conrad's critics find hard – understandably hard – to accept. Yet such a rejection, drastic and Utopian although it may seem (or even be), lies very close to the heart of many twentieth-century writers. We find it in the work of men as diverse as Robert Graves, Wyndham Lewis, Ezra Pound and T.S. Eliot, D.H. Lawrence, Ford, and even Hart Crane, who may be said to have sought to defeat technology (in *The Bridge*) by embracing it too wholeheartedly. The passage also demonstrates the profundity of Conrad's pessimism: the inescapable implication is that the male is bound to fall, because his naturally religious curiosity about his own existence is tainted by the quest for power which he brings to it. Gould's fall, apart from his treatment of his wife, consists of endowing the mine with a personality, and then subordinating his slaves, the mine workers, to this fiction. The one way to explore the paradise of snakes is to do it erotically. But Gould refuses this, as the narrative makes clear. And so Mrs Gould is denied love, which her husband doubtless thinks of as the mere satisfying of an appetite for affection. His romance is with emptiness, instead of with his wife.

Decoud, in part a self-portrait of the artist as a young man, is an exhausted decadent: the writer as he should not be. But, and here Conrad's irony is peculiarly harsh, he is also (paradoxically) the imaginative writer he is forced to be (he actually is a journalist), sceptical of "worldly things", possessed of a studied cynicism, guiltily "above politics". It is Decoud who emphasises that aspect of the novel which points to the fatal weakness of human beings when it comes to their realising their own fully individual, unique, existence. He is the opposite of Gould in that he is positively anti-'idealistic'; but his nihilism, though more sophisticated, is tested and found to be no better. The true love of a woman can sustain him no more than Emily's can sustain Gould. He kills himself in order to avoid facing his own individuality, an unknown quantity which terrifies him. "After three days waiting for the sight of some human face, Decoud caught himself entertaining a doubt of his own individuality." The fulfilment of that doubt is what he really wants: he can then merge with, and lose himself in, nature. "In our activity alone do we find the sustaining illusion of an independent existence as against the whole scheme of things of which we form a helpless part". Gould uses the silver to justify his death-in-life; Decoud uses it to keep himself "swallowed up in that immense indifference of things". It is a further piece of irony that Decoud's blueprint for Sulaco, drawn up by him to impress the girl he loves, and never believed in by him, should be put into effect when Sulaco secedes.

Yet Decoud's defeat is not unsympathetically presented. For the novel must be seen as "a monument to futility". Decoud's straightforward solution is infinitely less ugly than Gould's hypocritical one. Gould, even as Holroyd's evil lackey, tries to smash nature, the paradise of snakes, with power and money; Decoud at least tries, mystically and misguidedly and in a cowardly way, to become one with nature. He never descends to the depths – the "modern heights" of a "free-market hero" – reached by Gould, the 'progressive' capitalist: "a man haunted by a fixed idea is insane... may he not bring the heavens down pitilessly upon a loved head [his wife's]?" Decoud has a self-awareness that Gould, as a materialist, cannot afford; his scepticism matches that of his creator. To some extent he is twentieth-century man, intelligent but denied any faith in the universe or his own existence in it by science and reason – we feel that Decoud would have been worth saving. In the first phase of his existence Decoud has been a Parisian, a Baudelairean dandy manqué. But in the second he is in love: he tries to mock himself, but cannot altogether succeed. At one point he is shown with "incredulous surprise in his eyes" at his own state of being in love. Could it be that he only pretends that he mocks his plans for the Occidental Republic? He sees more deeply than anyone except for Emily Gould and Monygham; he can analyse both Nostromo and Gould with intelligence and accuracy. Into Decoud, with his "fatal touch of contempt for himself", Conrad invests his own guilt as a man capable of issuing blueprints for the future, but unable to stay on in order to sustain and humanise them. The self-willed death of such a man – and in it we see a prophecy of Conrad's own future self-willed death as a writer – is felt as a loss: Conrad does recognise that the intelligent and creative person's withdrawal from the political arena is a loss. But how otherwise could he perform his suicidal 'business'?

Decoud is the intellectual, who "lives in his head", turned false mystic by fear, only half defeated; his companion Nostromo, by contrast, is the instinctive, the 'natural' man, who "lives in his guts". His luck, his good fortune, is to be a foreigner, an Italian, who is trusted by everyone: he is 'our man' to everyone else. His sense of himself is at first entirely dependent upon how he appears to others – he has thus lost the inner core of himself, shares none of Decoud's solitude. He depends upon a perhaps ultimately insane vanity. But he is superstitious. And understandably so, for his reputation is a myth, as his betrayal (if it can really be called that: that is how the worthy but bovine Captain Mitchell would look at it) of trust clearly demonstrates. Decoud, given his chance alone with nature in the Placid Gulf, chooses death.

But Nostromo chooses to became an individual: he changes his name and lives by stealth on the stolen silver, giving himself airs as a rich tradesman where he was once chief troubleshooter. He dies by an 'accident'; but he is in truth guilty of exactly what old Giorgio Viola suspects the intruder (whom he thinks to be Ramire), to be guilty... his bad faith explodes in his face: he hates the silver, and Mrs Gould tells him – when, as he dies, he confesses to her – that she does: "I, too, have hated the idea of that silver from the bottom of my heart".

However, when the excited Monygham, "almost brutally in his impatience", asks her what Nostromo has said, she replies, steadily, "He told me nothing".

Thus the 'incorruptible' symbol of virtue is seen to be, simultaneously, the source of evil, and is denounced. (Better to be a MacWhirr than to be mixed up in things like that!) The only hope that is visible in the novel is that higher aspirations do exist, are thought of, do serve as a basis for action – as well as, in Gould's case, to exploit and bolster up evil and hubristic ways. "Human beings", we might well say, "need virtue to pursue evil ways: there must be something in it!"

A few, frightened by Conrad's bleakness, have tried to find here more hope and optimism than is actually signified. Conrad never again attempted to work on so large a scale. It would thus be salutary for a conformist or an optimist – a cultural official, let us posit, anxious to promote Conrad as a great British optimist – to discover in *Nostromo* some indication of a political programme in which Conrad believed, something akin to the programme to which our official's salary commits him. And it is thus further salutary, if scarcely acceptable, to point out that the Conrad of *Nostromo* did not believe in "that kind of thing", that he has indeed been struggling against time and illness to show it up as worthless. And yet was he not, once more, being strangely 'modern'? An increasingly large number of people have now reached the conclusion that any solution to the problems of human evil must transcend what hitherto has passed as 'politics' as right, left or centre? Yet the dying Nostromo, 'our man', the one chosen to give this massive book its title, may hold some kind of wise secret. When Emily

Gould tells him that she too has hated the silver from the bottom of her heart, he answers with a truism, but then offers to tell her where the treasure is: "To you alone… Shining! Incorruptible!" She is "appalled", and refuses. He is of course offering her material wealth, riches, or knowledge – but *may* he not also be offering her a wisdom of which she dares not avail herself? There is at least a hint of this, though it cannot be said to amount to more than a hint. Nostromo came into contact with his own true nature when he decided he had to steal the silver. In the famous passage which ends the seventh chapter of the final section, when he awakens, he is momentarily "free from evil":

> At last the conflagration of sea and sky, lying embraced and still in a flaming contact upon the edge of the world, went out. The red sparks in the water vanished together with the stains of blood in the black mantle draping the sombre head of the Placid Gulf: a sudden breeze sprang up and died out after rustling heavily the growth of bushes on the ruined outwork of the fort. Nostromo woke up from a fourteen hours' sleep, and arose full length from his lair in the long grass. He stood knee deep amongst the whispering undulations of the green blades with the lost air of a man just born into the world. Handsome, robust, and supple, he threw back his head, flung his arms open, and stretched himself with a slow twist of the waist and a leisurely growling yawn of white teeth, as natural and free from evil in the moment of waking as a magnificent and unconscious wild beast. Then, in the suddenly steadied glance fixed upon nothing from under a thoughtful frown, appeared the man.

He becomes a man as soon as he begins to think. The implication is that man is fallen, and cannot escape sin. And although the 'incorruptible' stuff paradoxically ensured that Nostromo's existence was a corrupt one, it became real in a way that it had not been before when he had been, not Fidanza, but simply 'our man', a mere reflection of the rest of humanity, an idea of the mob's. He has felt the 'treasure' of being himself, but has in so doing become a criminal, has had to conceal the source of his wealth, the fountain of his new, 'authentic' reputation. Conrad seems to suggest, with fine irony, that an individual involves criminality – and certainly to the 'real anarchists', individuality is the worst of all. In this notion the paradox of retaining true individuality and yet being a part of society – being properly 'bound together', as the word religion itself suggests – is touched upon. Emily is "appalled" at – or too wise to consider, in her understanding of her husband – the chance of such, and rather goes to her life of loveless disillusion without it. Yet Nostromo himself did learn to love, even if he could not admit which daughter he really loved, when he lived his false life on the hidden silver. And though his death is the result of a mistake, there is a wrenched justice in it: Giorgio shoots him because he thinks he is Ramirez – and he wants to do what Ramirez wanted to do; but Giorgio would not have shot him for it, had he known who he was. The truth of things is available to us, Conrad is saying, but through crooked, unexpected and devious ways. It will certainly make us suffer. The justice of Nostromo's death is undeniable; it can hardly in itself be called tragic; but it is tortuous. The Conrad protagonist is never a true hero, never one with whom the reader is allowed wholly to sympathise.

Mrs Gould is perhaps the one exception in all Conrad's fiction; but she is also one of his most thoroughly defeated creatures, since she ends up bereft of the personal consolation of children or even love – without hope of any kind. She is the only character except Monygham (who is, after all, a doctor) who actually cares for others in a practical manner.

Much has been written about Conrad's 'politics', and, as we have seen, he has been presented both as reactionary conservative and as an "unconscious Marxist'". All that remains to be said, to be repeated, on this subject, is that he was neither. As a man of his particular experience – as a Pole whose father had been a revolutionary poet, as a seaman, and as a poverty-stricken author watching the high financial success of inferiors – he sourly distrusted the new to an extent that makes even his friend the comparatively insensitive Galsworthy look like an angry leftist.

But he was in fact, as I have remarked, a Flaubertian liberal – that is, a disillusioned liberal who put imagination above political philosophy. The good works of Mrs Gould, as Conrad presents them to us, make it evident that he was no paternalist: racial equality and social justice were conditions he thought desirable: but he found them relatively pointless in this sort of world. Nor did he trust democracy to bring them about. However, there is no evidence whatsoever that he believed in, or advocated, any other system. In fact, as a person rather than writer, he wavered between despairing nihilism and stoical acceptance: he simply rejected politics, on account of politicians, wishing to put that good will which is not accessible to 'practical politicians' in its place. But he angrily saw that this, too, was impractical, and so felt guilty. His work, controlled above all, does offer a substitute: a truth-obsessed vision. But he felt a doubt about the usefulness of this. And he was justified. For was he not, like so many major (and minor) writers, an exceedingly selfish man?

How widely acceptable is such a vision? Conrad did not possess the artistic self-confidence of his (personally) much 'coarser' master, Flaubert, who thoroughly enjoyed cocking snooks at life, manners, and critics. The sovereign symbol of both writers' care for others, their social conscience, is feminine: women finally defeated by corruption. The more robustly cynical Flaubert could also portray a character, a woman (in *Un Coeur Simple*) who is *undefeatable*; Conrad could never have achieved so lyrical and positive a piece of writing. The nearest he can come to this is in the sentence describing Emily Gould as a vivid figure in "clear patches of sun": a moment in his gloomy work that has the effect of a shaft of bright light suddenly illuminating the dark cellar of his Polish imagination. A few men have known women like that. Flaubert gives us a portrait of a soul so innocent that it is incapable of registering this world as a dark place at all. Of course she is *ignorant*, too – but Flaubert was not. In Conrad's work he struggles, like Whalley, the half-blind captain in the *The End of the Tether*, to *pilot* his way through a murk of perpetual evil.

We have to acknowledge a quasi-pathological element in Conrad's view of life; but he saw fit to 'correct' it on 'moral grounds', and so he never reached a level of cheerfulness. Such never really breaks in upon him. He was almost always near to a state of clinical depression. When one thinks of Conrad the man's depressed portrait of himself, one irresistibly thinks of Verloc lying on the sofa, in *The Secret Agent*, seeing his wife raising the carving knife to stab him, but too lazy, almost too contented in his sloth to prevent her. Conrad put rather more of himself into Verloc, the grubby agent, informer, killer and salesman of pornography, than is generally conceded: that was how, emotionally, and with typical gloom, he rated the role of the imaginative writer who feels compelled to retain his integrity – at the expense of others.

Apart from Mrs Gould, Monygham is the only other 'saved character' in *Nostromo*. He certainly cannot be seen, as can Emily, as 'likeable'. Yet he is both heroic and modest. He is also the kind of idealist who is at least capable of constructive love. It has been said that Monygham naturally "disbelieves in the honesty of everyone else". This is a misreading. For not only does he believe in the honesty of his beloved Emily: he alone has the sensitivity to realise that Emily's life "has been robbed of all the intimate felicities of daily affection which her tenderness needed as the human body needs air to breathe". That delicate insight – which, with its "intimate felicities", bears cogitation – is not that of a dishonest man. It reminds us that Monygham has gained his sensitivity by being forced to explore the limits of his endurance. The insight very effectively underlines the tragic nature of Emily's disillusionment – incidentally demonstrating how sexually precise the earlier novelists could be when deprived of the opportunity to be explicit. Gould, we are here being told, is as selfish as a lover as he is a human being: he takes his pleasure heedlessly from the woman he is supposed to love; she is given no chance to reciprocate at an emotional level to a man who "relieves himself" – accompanied no doubt by those pious clichés whose falsities all women still in possession of their femininity are able, sadly and tiredly, to discern. This aspect of Emily's tragedy, intimately linked as it is with Gould's corruption, cannot be over-emphasised. Monygham is naturally conscious of it, and his own integrity – sour, even squalid, though he may be – is never entirely dissolved in the acid of corruption of that degenerate form of life, and subject of so many cerebral treatises, called politics. There are features of Conrad himself in the bitter, damaged but wise and reluctantly imaginative and empathetic doctor. The means of his redemption are, once more, ironic. Believing himself, over-modestly, as only too well cast for the role of 'traitor' (because of his earlier 'confession' under excruciating torture), he deceives Sotillo with confidence, and thus saves Emily and much else. True, he is indifferent to the fates of Decoud and Nostromo; but not more or less so than the author is, to characters of whom he is about to dispose. Conrad took his characters more seriously than most politicians and their accomplices take those whose external destinies they control. Another resemblance between Conrad and his crippled doctor is that both have been forced into scepticism. Can a serious modern author – one who is not simply an entertainer, or who has given up to a system (as Mauriac did when he decided to allow his church to take over the destiny of his characters) – whatever he may think he thinks about his intellectual commitments, manage, in the act of composition, *not* to be a sceptic? Can any honest doctor, in making his all-important diagnosis, afford not to maintain an open mind? Yet it is the twisted sceptic, the ruthless cynic, who saves Emily. He alone shows true wisdom in dealing with the barbaric sadist Sotillo. Like a writer, he cannot afford to be swayed by lucubrated moral niceties. But Monygham is spared what would have been the final justification of his cynicism: he is not allowed to sink into too self-indulgent a morass of bitterness.

That is Emily's gift to him in return for his devotion: he begs her to tell him what the dying Nostromo has said about the treasure, but she will not tell him. "He did not believe Mrs Gould. But her word was law... Even before that woman... he had been defeated by the magnificent Capitaz [Nostromo]... the man who had lived his own life on the assumption of unbroken fidelity, rectitude and courage". The ultimate wisdom, then, lies with Emily Gould – who won't disturb things. And what remains is just this: that some of Conrad's readers have known, or are, Mrs Goulds. She did not come from nothing nor nowhere.

Like most writers of his calibre, there was an aspect of writing of literature, which Conrad disliked with singular intensity. Writers disturb things (and people). Women of the sensitivity of Mrs Gould, though they lack the duplicity of politicians, seldom find this desirable: they are, in some way Conrad recognised but never understood, laws unto themselves. It is not without significance that his own wife, as evidenced by the obtuse memoir of him which she wrote and which was so deprecated by Edward Garnett, was no Mrs Gould.

V THE MAJOR WORKS (4)

The Secret Agent

In *The Secret Agent*, Conrad's next book, we have a simpler novel, and one which cost Conrad less effort: it came as a relief after the impossibilities of *Nostromo*. Altogether more consistently scornful, it is nearer to artistic perfection. He wrote in his 'Note' to it that it arose from "a period of mental and emotional reaction" following the publication of *Nostromo*. It is not as rich or as diverse in theme, but remains exemplary. Graham Greene, for example, who went into much the same sort of territory, never came close to matching it. It shows, in Conrad's own words, that "perverse unreason has it own logical processes". It is ironic from start to finish, both in tone and in plot. In it Conrad set out to parody the commercially successful melodramatic novel, so that it is comic in just the way Christopher Marlowe's farcical tragedy *The Jew of Malta* is comic. It is easy to see why, for so many readers of Conrad, it is the novel they *enjoy* most.

The Secret Agent has been called a sardonic sequel to *Nostromo*. At the end of the latter Conrad had made it clear how the state of Sulaco (the name of the revolutionary state of Costaguano) would 'evolve': his picture of the London of 1886 – but it was really the London of 1906 – is a cruel and mocking elaboration of this 'evolution'. Some critics have been misled, yet again, into believing that in it Conrad was expressing either life or right-wing views; most often he is attacked for giving 'unfair' or over-caricatured portraits of anarchists. That is missing the point. In every department of the book he is exploring, as he said, the perversity of "unreason". Norman Sherry, who has done so much (and done it so well and meticulously) to trace the sources for the novel, believes that the Home Secretary, Sir Ethelred, "escapes" the "macabre humour" which distinguishes the rest of the book! But there is nothing respectful in this disturbingly precise cartoon; the sheer fatuity of Toodles supplies the absurd context. However prejudiced the portraits of the 'anarchists' may appear at first sight to be, Conrad had to project himself imaginatively into their personalities and understand their points of view. They are essentially comic caricatures; only one, Ossipon, is an evil man. But the book as a whole presents them as no worse than their apparent adversaries, the politicians and the middle classes – and their servants, the police. He was not, he sarcastically wrote, concerned to "legitimise" any of them; but he added that his view of the "moral reactions as between the criminal and the police"

– that they were opposite sides of the same coin – seemed to him "at least arguable". That was taking things rather far in 1920, about a novel published in 1907. It could even be taken as an anticipation of a deeply shocking contemporary view of politicians: that they are polite psychopaths who put themselves forward, quite unqualified, as fit to solve problems of whose nature they have no inkling.

The Secret Agent, in almost all other respects the indictment of a corrupt society, is also the story of Winnie Verloc, told (as he asserted in his 1920 'Note') "to its anarchistic end of utter desolation, madness and despair". This arose from his infuriated, guilty reaction to family life: his own. He cannot be said to have hated his family, but he used his involuntarily bitter feelings to add venom to a contemptuous and cynical analysis of marital 'respectability'. Jessie, ill, learned in early 1906 that she was pregnant, and even suffered "a nervous breakdown of a sort"; Conrad, try as he would, could not help half-resenting a condition of which his appetites were the cause. She could never follow him where his imagination took him. Jessie was a good wife, who, rather like Winnie Verloc, dealt with her impossible husband by seldom saying anything ("Oh, yes! I know your deaf-and-dumb trick" Verloc tells Winnie). But he felt desperately guilty that he could not raise money to see to her needs without becoming "sick with worry and overwork". So in *The Secret Agent*, as Karl suggests, he "eliminated *his* family, which consisted of a much younger wife [as Winnie is with Verloc] and their young child. By making Stevie retarded, Conrad revealed another aspect of hostility, a measure of retribution for the son who must be supported and cared for". But that is only at the primitive level from which works of art obtain their momentum, and Karl should have added that in this way Conrad made sure of sublimating his ill will. In the event, under a concatenation of non-recognition, severe illnesses and shortage of money, he managed to take care of them – and of the new arrival, John, of August 1906. Borys, the elder son, was throughout this period so ill that he looked likely to die.

He knew all the time that it was going to be a novel, but pretended to Pinker – who liked short, quickly saleable fiction – that it was a story soon to be finished. It was called *Verloc* in its early stages, and he was working at it in January 1906. He may even have persuaded himself that it actually would turn out to be a short story. But he could not make the speed his purse needed, and by September, the month after John was born, had managed only 45,000 words (*The Secret Agent* is, in total, over 100,000 words). It was due to be serialised in 'Ridgeways: A Militant Weekly for

God and Country' (an exquisite spur to Conrad's mockery and irony – though the serial differs greatly from the volume) towards the end of that year. Conrad sent this early section to Galsworthy, who was predictably alarmed by what he deemed to be, its "Zolaesque" style. That was in a sense promising, and Conrad told Galsworthy that "attacking anarchism" would have to be left to a hand "more robust than mine".

He called the book "purely a work of imagination", and was very guarded as to his sources. Actually he wove the tale around a tissue of disparate facts, some of them well separated in time. The novel transcends all these facts, but Conrad (conscientious, like Hardy, in this respect), required justification for any state of affairs he depicted. *The Secret Agent* could hardly exist without Dostoievski – though Thomas Mann exaggerated when he declared that Stevie was "inconceivable" without *The Idiot* – just as it could hardly exist without Dickens. It employs the technique of caricature more consistently than any of the other novels; and its comic sense resembles Dostoievski's more than any other writer's – before or since. Stevie does in one or two respects resemble Myshkin of *The Idiot*, though he is not at all like him; likewise the Professor owes something to Kirilov. Clearly Conrad had been much taken with Dostoievski's *The Devils*.

But Dostoievski was a Russian, and Conrad could not like Russians – probably never even tried to like them. He did not want to understand that every individual Russian was not responsible for the Russian treatment of Poland, or for the death of his parents. So he would never admit to the influence, which was in fact strong (most particularly in *Under Western Eyes*).

One of the reasons why Conrad took so much of his detail from newspapers and recent history was, then, simply because he felt defensive about the growing influence of Dostoievski. The other reason, more important, is that he felt defensive about his cynical attitude or what he felt would be taken as such. *The Secret Agent* is remarkably 'modern' in the jaundiced view it takes of political activists, respectable politicians, conscientious policemen, and even of the sacred institution of marriage. While it is an atrocious error to take Conrad as a disguised Marxist *à la* Balzac, it is equally wrong to see him as, even in this book, a true reactionary – however he chose to talk to his country friends. When, he said he was simply attending to his business, what he meant was that an author had a right to the autonomy of his imagination. He knew from the start that he was presenting a savage and wounding attack upon the society of the Britain which had taken him in; he therefore felt easier in his mind for having a set of facts behind him – even if, characteristically, he refused to be specific about the amount of research he had done.

The anarchism, idealism and romanticism of the younger Conrad were well hidden, and had been well battered, in the elder. But they did not die in him. They lived vigorously on in his fiction, although they were subdued by depression and a world-weary cynicism. He used to complain that Hardy was just as pessimistic as he, but sold better. But Hardy was not as pessimistic: he was a lyric poet. However, the power of a satire as scarifying as this novel must arise from a belief in some different state of affairs. Conrad did share Marx's view that men and women should not be treated as merchandise. But he did not share his historical determinism, and still less could he share the 'dialectical materialism' of his followers, such as Engels and Plekhanov (who first used this term).

In 1906 Conrad was at the end of his tether. The almost sacred Mrs Gould can only now be Winnie Verloc's grotesque but unselfish mother; the corrupt materialist Gould can only be the psychotic nihilist, the Professor. Here we have a public world, not a private one. Even what is private is horribly unilluminated by the particular or the individual – which is precisely reflected in its own underworld: the subverters of society supported by its own pillars, or by a series of stupid upper-middleclass women (as in Ossipon's case), policemen who enjoy the 'manhunt' but who regard the ordinary criminal as one of themselves. The least unattractive man in the entire story, barring the retarded Stevie, acts as he does only because he wishes to defer to his whining and hypochondriac wife, whom he loathes. The pathetic heroine is party to a bargain which makes her into an unhappy, unwilling prostitute. Underlying the whole, and all the more powerful for never being explicitly stated, is a seamy lust: the greedy and disgusting fraud and robber, Ossipon, and his women and his treachery; the indolent Verloc who "can't go to Europe" because, as his wife slyly reminds him, he'd "miss her too much"; the Professor who walks the streets with his fingers round an indiarubber ball which will blow him and those near to him into smithereens. It is no wonder that in those days Conrad felt he needed a tissue of facts to reveal "The horror! The horror!" In our own time most of the people, except when they are in a state of shock – have assimilated it: protected from it, swaddled by the cottonwool of the media.

The Secret Agent is set in 1886, but its central incident is based on an actual occurrence: the Greenwich Bomb Outrage of 1894. It is instructive to learn how Conrad exploited the events for his fiction. He did not like 'outrages' any more than the vast majority of us, but his despair led him into a certain nihilist relish when they happened (the mood is also in Hardy's "Convergence of the Twain", about the Titanic disaster). He would have understood Turgenev's habit of possessing and studying photographs of executed terrorists. Perhaps Turgenev looked for resemblances between them and their executioners. This is one of the themes of *The Secret Agent*. Sherry has shown that the book is based far more precisely upon the Greenwich incident than most people had supposed – or than Conrad wished to acknowledge. He was very sensitive on the point. While he did admit it to his publisher, Sir Algernon Methuen, in 1906, he denied it to a correspondent in 1923 (more securely a country gentleman by then): he said that he had been out of England at the time, and "never knew anything of what was called the Greenwich Bomb Outrage". In fact he was in London, at 17 Gillingham Street, completing his first novel, and of course had taken a delightedly morbid interest in it. He based this part of the novel on accounts of the affair he had read in the *Anarchist* newspaper and on some later pamphlets about it. Ford gave him special knowledge of anarchism, which he had gained through his cousins, the precocious children of William Michael Rossetti, who, although their father worked for the Inland Revenue, were splendidly allowed to run an anarchist paper from the basement.

Briefly, the facts behind the Greenwich affair were these. A young man called Martial Bourdin was found in Greenwich Park on a hill near the Royal Observatory, "in a kneeling posture, terribly mutilated", on the evening of 15 February 1894. There had been an explosion. Bourdin had set it off and in so doing had killed himself. He had blown off one of his hands: his guts were spilling from his body. In using this incident, Conrad was by no means unaware of its symbolic significance as an attack upon bourgeois science.

Bourdin had a brother-in-law called H. B. Samuels, who edited an anarchist paper. Samuels was, like Verloc, a police agent and, again like Verloc, he accompanied his unintelligent dupe to the park. Bourdin did not stumble (as Stevie did), but in some way set off the explosive he was carrying, which had been supplied by Samuels, acting as agent provocateur. Samuels had intended that his sister's husband be arrested for carrying explosive, and probably suggested that he "experiment" with it in Greenwich Park. Samuels, therefore, must be the source for Verloc (he may even have been working for a foreign embassy as well as for the police), although Conrad did not make Verloc resemble him personally. Anarchists were not responsible for the Greenwich Park incident; they were as frightened about it as they are in the novel.

The Conference of Milan to which Vladimir refers was held in late 1898. Nothing came of it, since Britain (as is often mentioned) resisted the notion of giving up her reputation as a haven for the oppressed.

For the four anarchists (Verloc is only posing as one) Conrad had specific models in mind, though it is doubtful if he had much interest in them as individuals. He drew not only on anarchist lore (some of it, as already mentioned, from Ford), but also on Fenian Irish Republican history. It should be remembered that the Fenians were not anarchist, but violently subversive activists.

Conrad's comic depiction of all the anarchists except for the Professor (who spends all day in his room working on "the perfect detonator") as incorrigibly indolent derives from popular sources. But he does not offer it at all in the spirit in which it was first presented in the columns of *Blackwood's* under the name of the literary critic Charles Whibley, for whom the anarchist was an "indolent monster, diseased with vanity, whose first and last desire is advertisement". Sherry states that Conrad's own insights are "similar to those of, and perhaps derived from, *Blackwood's Magazine*". This is to do Conrad an injustice. Doubtless he was struck by the crude characterisation, but he knew that they were true of all anarchists (e.g. millionaires, whom he called "real anarchists"). He was portraying a particular, futile, group, known as anarchists: "sham" revolutionaries (as he put it to Graham, thus revealing a recognition of the real). He also wrote that there had been moments in the writing of the book when he himself had been himself "an extreme revolutionist".

Sherry insists that Conrad "deliberately excludes the human and intimate aspects of his historical originals in order to condemn the anarchists by a caricatural presentation". Now that is a good-hearted point, to be taken seriously; but, as I have remarked, it is based on a slight misreading, or series of misreadings. Sherry is one of those who believes that *The Secret Agent* is an "anti-anarchist polemic". First, to return to the matter of the presentation of the 'establishment' figures: it does seem that Sherry has quite missed the cruelly pointed absurdity of the Home Secretary, and of his Toodles. He thinks the portrait is "delicate and chiding", and that it is closely based on Sir William Harcourt! Harcourt, who died in 1904, was ridiculous and pompous in manner and much caricatured in magazines; but he was also capable of giving an effective (and, as it happens, ironic) speech. Conrad may have had his manner in mind in making fun of Sir Ethelred, but not his capabilities. Sir Ethelred, in a clearly Fordian device, is credited with wanting to introduce a Bill to "nationalise the fisheries" –

something the agitator Grahame might well have wanted to do; but there was of course no such bill. There is nothing "delicate" or "chiding" in Sir Ethelred's wanting from the Assistant Commissioner "no details", but "lucidity": he is, as Kirschner has remarked, no more than a "duffer".

The Secret Agent is far more than an anti-anarchist polemic: it is in its own creative way itself 'anarchist', since it is a satire on the whole of society. But Conrad would have well appreciated even Sherry's being taken in, too: he was himself ambivalent about his creative intentions, as his disingenuous 1920 "Note" demonstrates.

Karl Yundt, who does not play a large part, but is there simply as a 'type' to lend credence and substance to the group with which Verloc associates himself in order to carry out his duties efficiently, is a burnt-out advocate of murder. Conrad clearly relishes his expression of Yundt's savage intentions, just as Zola, the paradigmatic naturalist, relished his descriptions of low life. "Can't you smell and hear the hide of the people burn and sizzle?" Quite so: Pinker, bank managers, and those who would not buy Conrad's books. There is no reason to suppose that Conrad himself did not agree with Yundt's last words in the book: "They are nourishing their greed on the quivering flesh and the warm blood of the people – nothing else". It is just that he did not (of course) "like Yundt", and would not have cared to express himself thus in conversation. Conrad did not believe in stock political solutions, whereas the chief model for Yundt, Johann Most, did. But it is significant that Most, who was often imprisoned, never used dynamite – he just talked about it. When, in his 1920 "Note", Conrad wrote of a "brazen cheat exploiting the poignant miseries of mankind always so tragically eager for self-destruction", he can hardly be accused of being unsympathetic: the people, he is saying, in words which would have alarmed his Sir Ethelred, do have miseries. Nor does he exclude himself from any tragic eagerness for self-destruction. To argue, as Sherry does, that Conrad is childishly finding reasons for a hatred of anarchism is to miss the point: he is saying that this murderous type, usually himself not even a murderer but only a blood-curdling agitator, is a *cheat*.

In Michaelis, Conrad presents a more sympathetic, albeit pathetic, even ridiculous, type. It strains one's sense of proportion to see this bloated and suffering figure as anything other than a sad innocent. Sherry makes much out of the fact that Yundt has gout and that Michaelis (like one of the most famous of all real-life anarchists, Bakunin) is overweight and bloated after his twenty years in prison (for a murder with which he had little to do, and did not even know had occurred) – Conrad is here making a marginal comment upon 'justice'. This, Sherry believes, helps to ridicule them. But he forgets that Conrad her/himself had gout, that Jessie was overweight and bloated, that every author writes parts of himself into his characters ('bad' and 'good'). He would not have thought of the gout and the bloatedness as being so much 'ridiculous' as 'futile'.

Michaelis, like Yundt, is based not on an anarchist but on a Fenian called Condon, who was unjustly sentenced to life imprisonment for a crime he did not commit, but who had the integrity to declare his opposition to the government at a time when he might have obtained mercy by feigning repentance: clearly Conrad wanted to present Michaelis as a man who would not hurt a fly, and who had paid the price for expressing his honest opinion. But he is, as Conrad called him, a "grotesque incarnation of humanitarian passion". Is he any more so, however, than his creator felt himself to be: bitter, pressed for money, surrounded by threats of illness, afflicted by the swellings of painful gout (which releases toxins affecting the temper)? Could mankind do without Michaelis's absurd and idealist vision any more than it could do without the terrifying impartiality of the autonomous imagination? Conrad never pokes fun at Michaelis, though he does at Sir Ethelred.

The Professor fascinates us as he fascinated Conrad. He is "incorruptible"! Conrad told Graham that while the other characters were "shams" he had not intended "to make him despicable". This would surely surprise both admirers of Conrad's (alleged) reactionary politics, and Sherry, who believes him to be "unfair to anarchists". The Professor famously says that if he is given "madness and despair" (in which Winnie Verloc's story, Conrad himself tells us, ended) then it will provide him with a lever to move the world. "I wanted," added Conrad to Graham, "to give him a note of perfect sincerity". The Professor, too, is an inevitable part of the society which Gould will generate in Sulaco; but he will lack Gould's capacity for rationalisation.

But, as to 'anarchists' at all: the Professor himself is not one, and it is a moot point as to whether any of the revolutionists in *The Secret Agent* are true anarchists. We cannot be sure how much Conrad knew about the anarchists of his time. Proudhon wanted peaceful change; Blanqui wanted a violent seizure of power; Bakunin took Blanqui's line. But all these men, and others, believed in the abolition of the state and its replacement by a system of voluntary cooperation between individuals gathered into (more or less) small groups. Many of them, then as now, were using the movement to express their own small neuroses and frustrations, to compensate for their sense of inadequacy, or to exercise their psychopathic tendencies. Yundt and Ossipon are excellent examples of such men. (Neither Blanqui nor Bakunin are clear and unequivocal examples.) But Michaelis, although he ought to have been taught a lesson by his experiences, cannot be classed with this type. Nor can the Professor. The Professor is essentially a criminal nihilist who does not believe in the possibility of cooperation. He is fuelled by rage; the single idea in his head arises from rage, not thought. One wonders about his parents.

The marvellously named Ossipon, coward and apostle of 'science', has no known source; his ideology closely resembles any Dawkins, any contemporary proponent of the "scientific millennium". For his psychology Conrad required a parasite: one who thrived on anarchism without giving anything to it, or particularly believing in it. He is probably a pimp, and certainly he lives off women. His strongest instinct is that of fear, closely followed by a principled indolence; whether his lustfulness is as powerful as his desire for money is an academic question, since he obtains money by the exercise of lust. The portrait of him can in no way be said to carry any condemnation of anarchism. But in that of Vladimir we do see an unmistakable indictment of what passes for diplomacy. Both portraits in any case carry serious implications for the human condition itself – that it can produce such creatures. And so, more or less, does every other portrait in the novel. There is no 'saved character'. True, the unnamed mother of Winnie Verloc is 'saved', and Stevie is; but the reader only has to contemplate their circumstances, their intelligences, their fates, to gain a hint of Conrad's state of mind as he wrote the book. And he was not thinking of how much he hated anarchists.

Here all the revolutionists depend in one way or another on the representatives of 'law and order'. What kind of law, what kind of order? This, and not how awful anarchists are, is the theme of the book. No one is even prepared to stop the Professor, though this might easily have been done without too much difficulty. The top stratum of society needs him: he manufactures indignation. For the Assistant Commissioner, Conrad, always anxious to have his facts about him, drew upon two previous occupants of this post: Sir Robert Anderson and Sir Howard Vincent. Anderson wrote *Sidelights on the Home Rule Movement* (1906), and Conrad even took a few details out of it. Vincent, for his part, also got a knighthood for his work, but owed much to a subordinate, an Inspector Williamson; in *The Secret Agent* the Assistant Commissioner takes the case into his own hands, and cuts Heat out. But Vincent, a fine crook the like of whom is badly needed in our own day, was known to have disguised himself (as the Assistant Commissioner does), and to have been a meddler. As for Anderson, he had the reputation of being "discreet", "silent" and "reserved" – "a mystery even to himself". He was regarded as a peculiarly "intuitive" detective.

Conrad's Assistant Commissioner, these details apart, is the work of his own imagination. He is, apparently, one of the least unsympathetic characters in the book; but it is notable that, for all his shrewdness, he is never moved by humanitarian impulses. As Chief of Police in some colony he had enjoyed the *"open air sport"* (my italics) of hunting criminals, and had been sorry when his nagging wife insisted on his returning to England. Heat needs to arrest Michaelis, but he does not want it: his wife's wealthy and influential friend would never forgive him, and that would make his own life even more unpleasant and difficult than it already is. He has no interest in the moral or humane aspects of the matter. He acts against Heat only to save himself trouble at home. If he takes the most intelligent and energetic series of actions in the book, then this is only because he is looking after his own interests. Were he possessed of any sort of principle whatsoever, then Conrad would have taken the trouble to indicate this; but not a single unselfish thought is recorded as passing through his cold, empty, intelligent mind. We can respect him only as one who has no wish to see a silly game continue. But what must he have been like at his "open air sport"? Heat, whose very reputation depends to a great extent upon Secret Agent Verloc (as the Assistant Commissioner puts it to himself) is portrayed as without character or feeling, the epitome of extreme stupidity, even if he is streetwise and shrewd in the way that senior policemen often are.

When Conrad, with some irritation, insisted that *The Secret Agent* was the story of Winnie Verloc, he meant it. The novel is far more uncompromisingly negative than its predecessor. There are no consolations in it. Mrs Gould of *Nostromo* was defeated, but not corrupted. Mrs Verloc is not of the same calibre, and certainly in no way 'saved'. Stevie is like the cab horse for which he feels so much compassion, but has not been granted the sense to save himself. Verloc is able to persuade him to place the bomb by telling him that he is acting in the interests of poor people and poor brutes. He does not want him to be killed, but when he is, he has no sense of loss – he thinks his wife needs no more than a "good cry". She, too, is oblivious to the boy's pitifully humane qualities. True, her love for him is heroic, and she has sacrificed her future for him. But she is no more than his helpless protector. When she learns of Verloc's carelessness, which has led to Stevie's death, she is awakened neither to his callousness nor to the hideousness of his work as a pornographer; she is shocked, like an animal, into murdering him. She calls Stevie innocent, harmless and loving (to Ossipon, who is interested only in possessing her, and then her money); but it is Verloc's peremptory instruction to her, to come to him to satisfy his indolent lust, that has shocked her – as she tries to tell Ossipon. She had traded her femininity to Verloc, who smothered it, in return for security for Stevie. She had easily been able to collaborate with him in what she thought to be his main business: as satisfier of masturbatory lust, keeper of a pornography shop. Her sacrifice cost her everything; as "Verloc's wife" she has been dead. Of that "life" she tells the unheeding Ossipon, "He loved me until I sometimes wished myself...''; the remark is unfinished But she has previously exclaimed, "You thought I loved him!" The missing word is "dead". So that, although benumbed, she has felt Verloc's lusts as anguish: her femininity, what there is left of it, becomes aware of itself only in the act of its own destruction. She tells Ossipon just this. Terrified of the gallows ("the drop given was fourteen feet"), she is now ready to trade herself to Ossipon, whom she really hates (as has been made clear earlier on). She calls him Tom; promises him that she won't ask him to "marry" her. We are presented with a human creature reduced to the idiocy of her brother, but terrified into the bargain.

Verloc himself is a powerful creation, and all the more so because he is a dull, wretched and amoral man. Conrad of course never at any point regarded himself as being as low, dull or self-deceiving as that, although; being a depressive, he often felt like that. But it was into Verloc and the Professor that he projected parts of himself in this novel.

Into the admittedly 'mad' ideas of the Professor – "the perfect anarchist", as Heat calls him, because he cannot recognise him, as he can his mere thieves, as a fellow creature – Conrad unleashes all his contempt for the mediocre. He makes him pitiful, yet he endows him with the power of the actual explosive which he carries around with him. He really is a starkly dangerous man – only Winnie, aroused, is as dangerous. He is dreadful in every sense of the word, just because Conrad (as, indeed, we all should) distrusted his own fury. The Professor truly disturbs Heat, and neither comes off better than the other in their encounter. The Professor is temporarily put off by the "unattackable stolidity of a great multitude", and Heat is reassured by the fact that this great multitude, thieves included, are "behind him". But neither the mad nihilist nor the unjust, complacent representative of law and order (who does not believe in order, since he wants to see the

Assistant Commissioner "fired out") is comfortable.

Conrad's projection of himself, or aspects of himself, into Verloc, is more subtle. At one level Verloc is a portrait of the lower-middle-class stalwart, whose false sense of values is exposed. This is most apparent in the passage describing his walk to the Russian Embassy. Watching, as he walks, the "town's opulence and beauty", he approves it: "All these people had to be protected". The "source of their wealth had to be protected". He would have rubbed his hands together, writes Conrad with withering irony, had he not been too lazy to make such a gesture.

Now the nature of Verloc's poisonous indolence is a truly original piece of characterisation. Here Conrad leaves his caricatural technique to one side. Verloc is piggish (he is called "burly in a fat-pig style"): his lustful indolence and complacency lead him to his physical death. He is literally too lazy, too insensitive to the rage which he has provoked, to protect himself in time; he is "paralysed" by this ferocity born "of the age of caverns, and the unbalanced nervous fury of the age of bar-rooms". Conrad's brilliant picture of this indolence, in Verloc a kind of amoral complacency and complete rationalisation of treachery, has its creative roots in the inertia which is felt, and must painfully be resisted, by every writer who has something to say beyond entertainment. Such inertia must precede the difficult – inevitably self-revealing, self-castigating – act of creation. It must even be the prelude to such positive outbursts of joy as we find in the best of Thomas Traherne or George Herbert. In creating Verloc Conrad was able to sublimate this state of mind, and to portray a man actually driven by a principle of indolence.

Yet, like many a man who resolves not to work for his living, Verloc actually works quite hard. The resolution not to work so often conceals a deeper neurosis: a refusal of honesty, a desire to be free without earning freedom. Such people do work hard because their activities are often of a criminal nature: they are anxious not be found out and inconvenienced.

Conrad's transmutation of his own situation into this truly horrible one in the novel is nothing short of wonderful, a true "objective correlative" – as the American painter Washington Allston put it, in a lecture, long before T.S. Eliot was heard of. It was only his almost terrible honesty towards himself that enabled him to achieve this transmutation. The notion of attention to 'business' was for him an ironic understatement. For in Verloc he gives us the most negative and self-questioning self-portrait, even on a metaphorical level, that it is possible for a writer to give. The writer as lazy opportunist revelling in an illusion of freedom; the writer as spy into the lives of others, as traitor to humane values, living off (because exploiting) the sexual lives of others; the writer as futile drudge, betraying the ideals he professes just as Verloc woodenly and complacently professes his desire to 'protect' opulence and luxury; the writer as destroyer of his wife's happiness, and as murderer of his children's – all in the name of pointless and unrealisable idealism; the writer who sees reality is no better than Verloc's shabby, treacherous and meaningless existence.

Conrad, with a gloomy zeal worthy of a gnostic against all the demonic obstacles to his salvation, reminds us that things really are just as difficult as all that. The effectiveness of this tragic satire has been earned. The structure of an entire society is exposed – and destroyed. It is shown to produce futility (as Conrad keeps saying, of the Greenwich incident), and to destroy the last vestiges of femininity. Those who actively oppose it are equally powerless. The real hero here is an idiot who blows himself up. The infected corpse of this society dragged out into the open is at all points shown to be have been violated – by pretence, egomania, greed, lust, hypocrisy, prostitution. Any so precise a guide to the processes of such violation appeals, always, to a ghost – a ghost, but a substantial one, of the elusive virtue of good will.

VI THE MAJOR WORKS (5)

Conrad and Ford: The Quarrel

The mood in which Conrad had written *The Secret Agent* had by no means cleared as he began *Under Western Eyes* – as a story called simply "Ramuzov" in December 1906. This mood had, on the contrary, like the pressures upon him, got worse. It was also during the writing of *Under Western Eyes* that the breach with Ford, initiated by Conrad, became final. Jessie, who could not help recognising the deep understanding between the two men, was more jealous of Ford than of any other of Conrad's friends; having him to stay became more and more difficult for Conrad. The effect of Jessie's hatred of Ford on her husband, the temptation offered by the notion of a quieter life without Ford – an energetic man who kept the attention of those who understood him perpetually engaged – have been much underestimated, as has the nature of their friendship.

Not so far back, in January 1905, he was still entirely reliant on Ford: with *The Rescue* in mind, he told Pinker ("confidentially") that "I can get Ford to help me in it a little – block out things and so on. He is here and getting better... My mind is freer than it has been for years..." And when, fourteen months later, he told Algernon Methuen that there "is only one man to whom I could open my confidence on that elusive matter" [a "very intimate" "definition" of his work]" he still meant, of course, Ford. Karl woodenly thinks this may have been Garnett, although Conrad wrote to Ford, in 1906, "I am certain that with no other man could I share the future" – in wandering around Montpelier "entranced".

But Ford's erotic and marital difficulties were daily increasing, and Conrad found that he could no longer offer him the emotional support he knew he needed, and from him deserved. This came to a head over their last collaboration, *The Nature of a Crime*, undertaken between May and July of 1906 and published in the *New English Review* in two parts in April and May, 1909, and then in volume form, with prefaces by both Conrad and Ford, in 1924. They published it under the pseudonym of Baron Ignatz von Aschendorf – something the fun of which would, as it is easy to recognise, have even more deeply offended a Jessie innocent of such literary "fun".

The Nature of a Crime is, certainly, mostly Ford's work, but, since its manuscript does not survive, it is impossible to say how much Conrad did to it. As with *Seraphina*, which formed the basis for the joint *Romance*,

Ford gave Conrad a manuscript to work over; it was (quite clearly) the subject of much animated discussion. Mainly, they wanted to raise some cash on it. In his preface to the volume publication of 1924, Conrad (close to his death and remembering the old closeness), concluded:

> After signing these few prefatory words, I will pass the pen to him [Ford] in the hope that he may be moved to contradict me on every point... I said "the hope". Yes, the hope. Eager hope. For it would be delightful to catch the echo of the desperate, earnest, eloquent and funny quarrels which enlivened those old days. The pity of it that there comes a time when all the fun of one's life must be looked for in the past!

All the fun of one's life! It is a revealing sentence in view of what happened to Conrad. We cannot blame him in the least for his final defeat. But he blamed himself. Impossible although it all was, the symbiosis with the obstinately incorruptible Ford had been irresistible. It had – since he deliberately chose to marry a women actually deficient in imaginative powers – saved his creative life. (This by no means implies criticism of Jessie, or in any way detracts from her excellent qualities.) *The Secret Sharer*, the story which Conrad wrote in November-December of 1909, just after Ford lost editorial control of *The English Review*, and Conrad knew he had let him severely down, imaginatively records Conrad's side of the Conrad-Ford affair.

There had been more trouble between Conrad and Ford than just Jessie's dislike and the older man's all too understandable mistrust of and even hatred for the intimacy he needed to keep going as a writer of integrity – one of the main themes, after all, of his life – but thus, alas, to remain poor and in need. It involved money, Ford, Arthur Marwood, Elsie Ford – now desperate to retain her husband – and Conrad as a fourth party dragged into it much against his will. It is an affair both complex and murky. When Conrad abruptly left the Pent in 1907 he put Ford, its landlord, into difficulties. He also owed Ford money. How much is not known, but the amount could have been large – by mid-1904, certainly, it was "almost £200", according to Robert Garnett – but it could have been more.

Ford possibly suggested to Conrad that he was hiding money he actually had in his possession, so as not to pay him when he was in need. Conrad over-reacted – and, indeed, might well have been concealing some cash he had in hand: he did have crippling expenses. The money was not then repaid, and Ford (characteristically) thought better of the matter. It was not in his temperament to take any such an affair seriously. Conrad was unable, or unwilling, to fulfil his financial obligations; so, when, later, a complicated row built up over a different matter, he seems to have been all too pleased to take sides, egged on by Jessie, against Ford. The business has never been written about even half satisfactorily because, while Conrad was zealous in his animadversions, Ford kept quiet.

The essence of what happened lies in Conrad's turn-away from Ford as "pilot-fish", to Ford's friend Arthur Marwood – to whom the former had introduced him. Jessie understood nothing of these affairs, and triumphantly wrote of Marwood as having "usurped [a revealing word, if she understood it] a place completely in my husband's regard and esteem". Marwood was indeed a brilliant and odd man, as one might expect of the person who sat for Ford's Tietjens. Conrad called him "the real Wise man of the Age", and got some wished-for solace in seeming to 'capture' him from Ford. But Marwood also sat for Ashburnham of *The Good Soldier*, and Ashburnham's fault is that his weakness for women leads him into both indiscreet ("scandalous") behaviour in a railway carriage, and treachery…

In 1908 Marwood (who was married) lent Ford £400 for an essential kidney operation on Elsie, thus putting Ford into uncomfortable hock with him. He subsequently made advances to Elsie, even reminding her that she owed her life to his generosity. Ford's attachment to Elsie was at this time weakening, in favour of the forty-five-year old writer Violet Hunt (who already desperately wanted to be Mrs Ford), so that he might have seen that as a perfect 'opportunity'. But Elsie desperately wanted to keep Ford, and so she made Marwood's behaviour public, possibly (but possibly not) exaggerating it. The truth of the affair may be very much more complicated: readers of *The Good Soldier* will be aware that when Ashburnham puts his arm round the nursemaid in the train and kisses her, he is "driven to it… by the mad passion to find the ultimately satisfying woman".

Ford knew that he was himself straying, and could (and was able to) sympathise with Marwood. But at the time, it appears – we have little documentation – he 'executed' Marwood (by means of cruel letters). That was Conrad's view: "I have seen a man guilliotined [sic]," he told Galsworthy, "30 years ago but it hasn't made me feel half as sick as the present operation. For weeks poor Marwood looked as if after a severe illness… [he is] incapable of any black treachery".

The point of these details here is not to stray into biographical commentary on Ford, but to emphasise the repentant nature of Conrad's feelings about the brutal way in which he treated Ford. Marwood, after all, although doubtless a remarkable man, was not Ford, and could not give him what Ford gave him. This was a manipulated transfer of affection, and done with a bad conscience.

The Secret Sharer

Conrad's guilt pervades *The Secret Sharer* and even, in part, *Under Western Eyes*. For Ford – who forgave Marwood – was in a bad position, and Conrad himself confided in Ford that he wouldn't "believe it's altogether without cause": but, he now warned Ford, he thought that he was "visiting... even grave failures of discretion in men who were [Marwood had at that point just told Conrad that he had cut off all contact with Ford – which in fact he renewed] your admiring friends with an Olympian severity... you have always sought to do good to people – that I believe – but don't fail in the other kind of generosity... indeed I didn't know why I should be wretched except from sheer affection". But the fact is that he did fail Ford, and knew he had done so: he could not handle the difficult situation, he simply abandoned Ford, took Marwood's side (as of course Jessie avidly and judgmentally did) when he could have avoided doing so. So he started to relieve his guilt by blackguarding Ford in all directions, and knew perfectly well that he was behaving badly because he wanted to rid himself of the burden of the only man who really understood him – in the sense in which Leggatt of *The Secret Sharer* tells the narrator that he "understood".

This is not a question of morals, or of who was 'right' and who was 'wrong', but of how the parties actually felt. Conrad, for the rest of his life except in some odd instances, continued to disparage Ford in terms that were, for him, suspiciously simplistic, morally orthodox and unironic. Ford remained silent. If he lost his temper and was unkind (or moralistic) to or about Marwood, then he changed his mind. We do not, for the most part, know what he actually wrote or said. He could be hysterical, and at this point, having only just recovered from a severe breakdown, probably was.

This brings us to the question: what is *The Secret Sharer* about? It is regarded as one of Conrad's masterpieces, and, furthermore, it offers us a key to a persistent theme in his work. He himself vulgarised it and simplified this theme when he turned into an 'eminent novelist' and his work declined: he called it, for the public, his "conviction" that

> "the world... rests on a few very simple ideas... It rests notably on the idea of Fidelity."

There is no need to sneer at this. But it is empty and unilluminating in the context of Conrad's subtlest work.

The story was suggested by an incident of which Conrad heard in 1880. The chief mate, Sydney Smith, of the *Cutty Sark* ordered a crewman, a black man, to do a job. The crewman refused and threatened him with a capstan bar – the mate wrenched it from him, and killed him with it. Smith then managed to persuade his captain, Wallace, to allow him to escape at the end of the voyage: he smuggled him onto an American ship. Eventually Smith was caught and, his victim being a mere rating and black to boot, he got only seven months. Captain Wallace killed himself.

In *The Secret Sharer* this is transformed. The story is only 'about Conrad and Ford' at a merely biographical level; at its profoundest level it is about comradeship – and, indeed, that Fidelity (and lack or impossibility of it) upon which the elder Conrad was forced rhetorically to fall. It is because of what the comradeship (for want of a better word) between Conrad and Ford stood for, in Conrad's mind, that I have put so much emphasis upon it. For in the *Secret Sharer* it is given a bitter and terrible twist.

In the story the "painstaking" chief mate, of "frightful whiskers", does not like or approve of his captain, the nameless young narrator who is somewhat of a stranger to himself, is uncertain of himself, and has only had his command for a fortnight. The narrator is ironic and scornful of the fact that this suspicious chief mate appeared comic in trying to "account for" a "miserable scorpion": "how it got on board and came to select his room rather than the pantry… and how on earth it came to drown itself in the inkwell of his writing desk". But the author, even the narrator, is one who knows about scorpions in inkwells! He takes the anchor-watch himself, to the mate's surprise, and observes another ship, the *Sephora*, "anchored inside the islands", whose intentions are uncertain and the subject of curiosity.

> The youngest man aboard (barring the second mate), and untried as yet by a position of the fullest responsibility, I was willing to take the adequacy of the others for granted. They had simply to be equal to their tasks; but I wondered how far I should turn out faithful to that ideal conception of one's own personality every man sets up for himself secretly.

While on this watch he finds a man hanging silently onto the rope side ladder which, by his own negligence, he has inadvertently left in place. The name of this man is Leggatt (*Le gât*, in French, is *quay steps*, a term with which as a former French sailor Conrad may well have been familiar – the way to the sea, and the way off it, the passage from one to the other), and he is from the *Sephora*; he was its chief mate, and he "killed a man". But the circumstances differ from Sydney Smith's manslaughter of the black man who would not obey him: we do not know those, but in this case there is no ambiguity in at least this sense, that the narrator, so far as he is concerned, *knows* that his "double", as he now already regards him, was "no homicidal ruffian". He knows it because he *is* Leggatt! The killing took place during a storm, and Leggatt does not know exactly what happened, only that he felled the half-crazy crewman "like an ox" and that they struggled, and that, when he came to, his hands were around his neck. "A sufficiently fierce story," he comments, "to make an old judge and a respectable jury sit up a bit".

The legal position is clear. Leggatt has to give himself up, and face trial. Nor can the narrator properly carry him on his ship. If he does so then he will be concealing a fugitive from justice. But he does carry him: he deliberately hides him, especially from his chief mate, and he allows him to swim away – after a risky manoeuvre near to the shore (he pretends that he is seeking land winds) which actually endangers his ship, and which puts his entire and more experienced crew into a panic. Not only that, but when the captain of the *Sephora* comes aboard his ship, in his search for the young fugitive now quite firmly identified by the narrator as his "double" he deliberately deceives him (Leggatt is meanwhile hiding by his side, as if sharing some deep joke), and even pretends to be "hard of hearing" – "What was the cause of it," the captain asks, "some disease?" – "Yes; disease," admits the narrator "in a cheerful tone which seemed to shock him". The captain continues:

> I've been at sea now, man and boy, for seven-and-thirty years, and I've never heard of such a thing happening in an English ship. And that it should be my ship. Wife on board, too.

The narrator asks the captain if he was very keen to hand the fellow over to the shore authorities.

> He was. To the law. His obscure tenacity on that point had in it something incomprehensible and a little awful... "He looked very smart, gentlemanly, and all that. But do you know – I never liked him... I am a plain man. You see, he wasn't exactly the sort for a chief mate of a ship like the *Sephora*"... I felt [adds the narrator] as if I, personally, were being given to

understand that I, too, was not the sort that would have done for the chief mate... I had no doubt of it in my mind.

One more detail of the killing is revealed by Leggatt. The captain claimed (to the narrator) to have given an order to reef a foresail, which saved the ship "by a special mercy I believe... I don't mind telling you that I hardly dared give the order". But Leggatt tells his double:

> He... whimpered about our last hope – positively whimpered... I just took it into my own hands and went away from him, boiling, and – But what's the use of telling you? You know!

And the narrator recognises that the

> same strung-up force which had given twenty-four men a chance, at least, for their lives, had, in a sort of recoil, crushed an unworthy mutinous existence.

He gives Leggatt his hat, to save him from sunstroke, and three sovereigns from the six that are in his possession, and makes an elaborate arrangement for him to escape to an island lying by Koh-ring, an imposing height, to a town "unknown to trade, to travel, almost to geography, the manner of life... an unsolved secret". As Leggatt makes his escape, the hat slips off – and it is only by means of it, floating in the dark water, that the narrator is able to judge his own exceedingly delicate and highly dangerous manoeuvre. He succeeds, to his crew's amazement and relief.

> Walking to the taffrail, I was in time to make out, on the very edge of a darkness thrown by a towering black mass like the very gateway of Erebus [entrance to Hades, a kind of quay-steps] – yes, I was in time to catch an evanescent glimpse of my white hat left behind to mark the spot where the secret sharer of my thoughts, as though he were my second self, had lowered himself into the water to take his punishment: a free man, a proud swimmer striking out for a new destiny.

But what did Conrad mean by this strange story about a young captain's involuntary decision to break the law? Had he, in his own command, been confronted with a similar circumstance, he too would have been obliged to tell the perpetrator, just as Captain Archbold did, "... You have killed a man. You can act no longer as chief mate of this ship". Archbold is over-legalistic, but any captain would need to protect himself. The narrator acts as he did because he "knows" that his passenger is not a "homicidal brute": that, indeed (he thinks) it was his courage in the face of probable death, not the whimpering captain's at all, that saved the *Sephora*. Just before he discovers Leggatt, he has been rejoicing

> in the great security of the sea as compared with the unrest of the land, in my choice of the unattempted life presenting no disquieting problems, invested with an elementary moral beauty by the absolute straightforwardness of its appeal and by the singleness of its purpose.

He soon learns otherwise.

Albert J. Guerard, a stimulating critic of Conrad, writes that many "critics and readers have liked *The Secret Sharer*, but few of them have cared to say what it is about." His own interpretation is interesting. It is, he rightly explains, "what is known as a 'double' story – and he cites Poe's *William Wilson* and Dostoievski's *The Double* as examples. "[Leggatt] is… the embodiment of [an] instinctive, more primitive, less rational self…" The narrator first experiences him as a "headless corpse!": therefore he is "a being without intellect". The narrator loses "all sense of personal identity": he "has descended, at his peril but for his final instruction, into the depths of the unconscious". And Guerard cites the "psychologist Jung, who was to argue… that only such a descent… can permit integration and enrichment of the personality". He concludes thus:

> The captain, having overcome his necessary but egoistic identification with Leggatt, and seeing him now as flesh rather than shadowy spirit, restores to the stranger his identity. In this sense, at least, each is now a "free man, a proud swimmer striking out for a new destiny."

Now it is true than Conrad may be and is often described as an intensely 'Jungian' writer, for reasons too obvious to need explanation; but this interpretation seems to be confused, and to impose theory on text. Here the sea is omnipresent, but there is little about diving into it – only at the end does Leggatt have to *jump* into it, but that, says the narrator, was for a destination in which he will be "hidden forever from all friendly faces, to be a fugitive and a vagabond on the earth, with no brand of the curse on his sane forehead to stay a slaying hand…". Had Conrad here meant to allude to the journey through the unconscious in quest of "integration" (admittedly a paramount theme in his work as whole), then he would have ended with his double, Leggatt, "committing suicide"; but that he has killed himself is the theory of many of his crew, and it is shown to be untrue. This story deals, rather with the life as it *has* to be lived: *outside* the unconscious, yet aware of it – the sea lies all through it, all around it, but its depths remain unpenetrated.

When Conrad came to write *The Shadow-Line* he used as its epigraph, remembering his years as bored young dandy looking at the surface of water to find meaning in his own reflection, Baudelaire's lines, *"D'Autre fois calme plat, grand miroir/De mon désespoir"* [At other times, great calm, great mirror of my hopelessness]. Here he deals with young men who have just passed this fatally narcissistic phase. The narrator brings Leggatt as near to the unknown land as he dares, risking his ship, but, in his solitary courage, becoming one with it:

> And I was alone with her. Nothing! no one in the world should stand now between us, throwing a shadow on the way of silent knowledge and mute affection, the perfect communion of a seaman with his first command.

This story deals not with any exploration of the unconscious, but with the perennial and mysterious theme of the double. In at least one Cabalistic tradition the great angel Metatron is a dual being with the devil Samael: they are condemned to inseparable companionship. This, in turn, links to the Gemini myth: in versions of it, one twin is white, the other black (Leggatt's hair, when the narrator first sees it, is black). One creates, the other destroys. The narrator is "innocent", Leggatt is hunted as a killer. One is the doctor, the other is the invalid. The narrator helps Leggatt in the trouble he is in. We are here in the "zone of contradiction": as a writer in symbols has succinctly put it, "in every individual object there are two formal components, one varying, the other unvarying... one of its faces bespeaks its individuality, the other links it with its species".

But Conrad thoroughly humanises this, turning it into a story which has been taken by many of its readers as straightforward adventure – with high suspense as to whether the suspicious crew, or Captain Archbold, will discover Leggatt; it has even been filmed (in 1952), as *Face to Face*, a two-part film with Crane's *The Bride Comes to Yellow Sky*. Leggatt is not the narrator's "unconscious half", he is his mysterious double – and that is how the narrator experiences him, seeing, for example, "himself" poring over a map as he goes down into his quarters, where he is concealing him.

The tale is rightly read, initially, as a piece of realism. Conrad has made it all perfectly 'possible'. Leggatt's escape route is impeccable in nautical terms; so is the rest. The only question the reader will ask if he discusses the realistic level of the story with himself, is: "Why did he go to all that trouble and danger to make this rescue?" But the answer can hardly be at that level of 'realism'. It is unlikely that any young captain would take such a risk – Conrad himself could not have done so. Yet the story has the force of psychological plausibility. So, on the next level of what is (as Guerard says) a story which operates on many levels, Leggatt, in some super- (not sur-) realistic sense, actually is the narrator. Leggatt is, as Guerard again rightly asserts, a somewhat dubious person. He got his job through influence and he did after all lose control and strangle a man. There is a case to answer and he prefers not to answer it in the face of "ordinary" people at a trial back at home in England. But the narrator, he understood – "wonderfully". And here he is, the narrator: he is Leggatt! He is compelled to help him, and he never questions his own actions – he is only ever afraid that he will be found out. Nor is Leggatt merely just his "irrational" self. *He is him!* The narrator never describes him except in terms of his being his double – there is only that one detail of the black head. But although the double is a persistent theme, in literature, art and even music, and although each man and each woman has his or her double, in some psychological sense, doubles do not exist in 'ordinary' life. They have to be very close friends, or lovers, and to exist in that terrifying – and, again, persistent – way that things that are 'impossible' *do* exist at some mysterious symbolic level. Here, by a neat device, Conrad demonstrates how it is necessary to rid oneself of them, or become mad – in this case, the double is not a lover, but a stranger who immediately becomes a friend. For it is upon those who "understand" (as "wonderfully" as Leggatt tells the narrator he understands) that we project our selves, our 'doubles'. The story, when deeply considered, tells of just such an experience: of how the narrator feels that the other man 'is' him, and so *must* say farewell to him.

Conrad and Ford: The Parting of the Ways

Conrad, a romantic man, did not marry one who could ever confuse him much sexually. Jessie, "no trouble at all", was never a "soulmate", never one of those for whom Shelley or the more scrupulous Hardy fruitlessly sought all their lives. Ford was. He "understood wonderfully". He knew about the paradoxes which poor Leggatt is not at all anxious to put before some old judge and jury in Norfolk. He had got his role "by influence" – he had been born into the pink of literature and had published his first works while still a boy. He was now in bad trouble. And Conrad, who was particularly virulent about Ford's lack of veracity, and megalomania, in the wild and condemnatory letters he wrote preceding his own severe breakdown, experienced just after completing his first draft of *Under Western Eyes* (January 1910), when he muttered in Polish, and the words of the burial service, and "talked to" Ramuzov and Haldin and the other characters he had just created, was about to "desert him": he would *no longer* "wonderfully understand".

Ford stood in his heart – Ford upon whom he had displaced so much of the spiritual side of his eroticism, Ford whose "wonderful understanding" had enabled him to write parts of *Nostromo* and had dug *A Mirror of the Sea* out of him – like a lover. Not a lover, but like one. Ford had gone off, and, deserting the Elsie (towards whom he – and Jessie – now exhibited the most bitter rage), with whose existence he had learned to come to terms, had gone off – to Violet Hunt! He knew Ford was making a mistake (he was; and he later suffered horribly from her revengeful tactics, when she even forged cheques in his name), and, above all, he was jealous. Here was Ford doing what he wanted to do! He was after a soulmate and at least he believed he had one! So *The Secret Sharer* is his secret tribute to the man with whom he was now in the process of making a final break. Never again would there be quite the old intimacy. Only once, perhaps, with the exception of that phrase from his last months – "all the fun of one's life" – did he forget his reserve: he was trying to write *The Shadow-Line*, but *The Good Soldier* – in which, for him, the atmosphere of much of the agonizing that they had shared together is reproduced with such priceless artistry – had reached him:

> Your cadences get into my head till I can't hear any of mine
> and become paralysed for days.

Those "cadences" were not just Ford's but Conrad's – and – Ford's: from the Pent in the old days.

VII THE LAST MAJOR WORK

Under Western Eyes

Under Western Eyes is Conrad's last unequivocally 'artistic' book, in which the need to speak truly (if despairingly) fully predominates over the struggle for survival, recognition, a reasonable financial life. It is the least good of his 'good books' – but a good one all the same. It is the least good because it depends so much upon Dostoievski, and because some – if not all – of the deep pessimism it expresses came out of a pathological state. It has been said that we have no 'proof' that Conrad knew *Crime and Punishment*, but the proof, or all but, lies in *Under Western Eyes*. Besides, Conrad did discuss the Russian writer, if exasperatedly – and discussion implies knowledge. It is fair to say that it is inconceivable that Conrad had not read Dostoievski's major works. Conrad seems to have wanted to outdo the hated Russian, and almost managed to produce his own gloss on *Crime and Punishment*. He had not minded being influenced by Flaubert; he could not bear to be so by Dostoievski, of whose "fierce mouthings" he violently complained. *Under Western Eyes*, which is narrated by a "Western teacher of languages", is very much Conrad's own book, but it does lie uncomfortably in the shadow of *Crime and Punishment*, and Ramuzov is Conrad's own Raskolnikov. Karl comments thus on the differences:

> The Russian showed his love for sinners, while Conrad demonstrated his distaste for nearly all human behaviour. For Dostoievski, sin, even the worse, was a form of energy and tied one to the workings of the universe; for Conrad, neither crime nor punishment could mitigate the fact that man was strung out on a puppet's existence. Man lived within a world of "Dreams, Hags, Magic Sleights."

This is just, but goes almost too far: the "sleights" are, after all, "magic" – they aren't conjuring tricks. Conrad himself said, too, "all creative art is magic" – and, again, he didn't mean conjuring. One remembers the words of Leggatt in *The Secret Sharer* to his savour, whose double he 'magically' becomes: "You seem to have been there on purpose". The true pessimist does not write at all. But *Under Western Eyes* is a (clinically) depressed and depressing book, and it does not have the manic energy or satirical zest that possess every page of *The Secret Agent*. And, while not at all simply 'about' the 'betrayal' of Ford, the loss of Ford, the end of "Excellency a few goats", it does incidentally reflect Conrad's crisis at many points.

The narrator of *Under Western Eyes*, the teacher of languages, gains his information from observation and from Ramuzov's own diary, given to him by Nathalie, Haldin's sister. Ramuzov, natural son of a Prince, and protected although not acknowledged by him, is a student who holds himself somewhat guiltily aloof from revolutionary politics. He is exceedingly ambitious, and so he is appalled when the fanatic Haldin, having just assassinated a minister of state, comes to him in his flat and asks him to shelter him – in the simple assumption that Ramuzov is so enlightened as to be wholly loyal to his cause. Ramuzov's generous conversation has not wholly separated him from the 'enlightenment' that is to get him into trouble with the other side – indeed, as he now to his horror discovers, he is revolutionary, the sort of man to whom a terrorist would naturally go!

The vivid description of the assassination itself has a characteristically Conradian touch. The victim is painted as both ridiculous and wicked, an entirely unsympathetic and cruel man, yet, just as he is murdered, he is seeing to his wounded coachmen – is viewed, therefore, in a rare act of instinctive humanity. But there is no sympathy for the Tsarists (after all, they had killed Conrad's parents). Ramuzov agrees to harbour Haldin, and even tries to follow out some of his instructions. But, when things go wrong, he goes to the Prince to report that Haldin has appealed to him for help. He finds himself a suspect for a time, but is finally shuffled off to Geneva as a secret agent. In Geneva he has the reputation of a revolutionary hero: when he and the Tsarist police had arrived at his flat, Haldin had already left, and so did not know who had betrayed him. Haldin (who is eventually executed) has written to his mother (who never, however, really believed in Ramuzov) and his sister telling them of how he tried to save him. The descriptions of the revolutionaries by whom the guilt-wracked Ramuzov is so repelled owe much to Dostoievski's *The Devils*.

He loves Haldin's sister Nathalie, and tries to break free by confessing:

> Victor Victorovitch Haldin... acting with, no doubt, noble-minded imprudence, took refuge with a certain student of whose opinions he knew nothing but what his own illusions suggested to his generous heart. It was an unwise display of confidence. But I am not here to appreciate the actions of Victor Haldin. Am I to tell you of the feelings of this student, sought out in his obscure solitude, and menaced by the complicity forced upon him? Am I to tell you what he did?

The revolutionaries burst his eardrums with billiard balls (the one who does this, the psychopathic Nikita, is revealed to be a traitor himself).

Ramuzov is run down and crippled by a tram he cannot hear.

This is a fine adventure (or 'spy') story, tightly written, but in its stark despair it more resembles a tragic *Bildungsroman*, in which Conrad was actually unfair to himself – but he was heading for a dangerous 'mixed state' (of mania and depression), for that breakdown of January-March 1910 which all but killed him – in representing himself as Ramuzov. He tries at first, to make Haldin seem immensely unreasonable and criminal; but his representation of the revolutionary ideals – but not the terrorist programme – and of the nature of Tsarist tyranny makes it clear enough that he was half-falling into his usual artist-criminal formula: we can see how, in his depressed mind, Haldin seemed like Ford, with all his impossible behaviour, his suicide threats, his demands for the primacy of the imagination, and inconsiderateness and lordly lack of tact with Jessie. Conrad had eschewed revolutionary violence, but had never actually condemned the notion of the desirability of the overthrow of the Tsarist regime on any grounds. And so, his poet-father having been something of a revolutionary, and having perished at their hands, he was able to identify them, symbolically, with the artistic cause. But it was a secret kind of identification, and one which he resisted. And it was complicated by the fact that he hated all Russians – Tsarists and revolutionaries alike.

Read with this in mind, the book makes it clear that he found artistic integrity an impossible goal – as, indeed, in its pure form, it is. But he had carried his guest so far and so intensively that he could go no further. Thus *Under Western Eyes* lacks any real resolution: the pathetic end of Ramuzov is Conrad's own end as a writer – Conrad's years of fame and recognition. From then onwards Conrad would turn to his old chivalric line: to the rescue of the damsel in distress, a theme first tried at in *The Rescue*, the book at which he worked spasmodically all his life, and which in the end turned out a failure. He had married Jessie, and had never even tried to rescue any damsel in distress. While in the profoundest possible sense we do owe to her – more than to Ford, who did not have to live every day with and minister to Conrad – all the major works he did write, she simply, and very precisely indeed, was not that sort of damsel, and did not have the kind of mind or heart that could be in the required kind of distress. Thus, paradoxically, she saved him.

As he continued with *Western Eyes*, an awful situation with Ford over *The English Review* was going on, and there can be no doubt at all that – difficult though Ford was about the handling of finances – he felt that he was deserting him when he deserved better. Indeed, he protested so much about Ford at just this time that his guilt feelings became obvious. But Jessie hated Ford, and he would have felt – ill and dependent upon her as he was – in a hole with her had he tried to defend him. Ford did bring disaster upon himself by failing to allow for what financiers were really like, perhaps for treating them as if they had no feelings; but in the *Review* affair he was at least 'in the right' over literature, and not one of the others – even Marwood – was really quite that.

Under Western Eyes does possess power, though – the kind of power that no reader, even a hostile one, can or tries to deny to Dostoievski. Ramuzov's anguish in Geneva, as Conrad describes it for us through the "Western eyes" of his narrator, possesses all the awful and awe-inspiring destructive power of depression itself – which has to be experienced, or at least seen, to be believed. The confused 'highs' of such a 'mixed state' as Conrad experienced almost immediately upon finishing the novel function as no more than nature's way of keeping the victim alive. Nor had Conrad ever been subject to violent manic attacks – or, rather, he had been, but he had been able to sublimate them into frenzied descriptions of his wild imaginary world.

The nature of Ramuzov's end should not escape notice. Getting weaker every day, not likely to live long, he lives in Russia, tended "unweariedly" by the "Good Samaritan", Tekla, who had wanted to save him and could have done if he had not been deaf. He is called upon occasionally by those passing through because he is "intelligent, has ideas... talks well, too".

VIII THE DECLINE

Meyer's Interpretation of the decline

This essay, a selective – some will say too boldly selective – introduction to Conrad, is bound to end with a discussion of his 'decline'. This decline, or alleged decline, forms an important part of his general reputation. Should it? Some authors, like Shakespeare (apparently, although he may have had poems in his drawer which his wife angrily destroyed), give up, retire, or become senile. Others, like Dickens, die in full harness, a major work uncompleted. But Conrad's fiction is widely held to have fallen off in mid-career, just after, to be precise, *Under Western Eyes*. This is (approximately) my own position; nor is it a lonely one. But F. R. Leavis, in *The Great Tradition*, influentially sought to rehabilitate Conrad's later fiction by means of his praise of *Victory* (1915), and, really, the argument stands or falls on that book.

The 'Leavisite' argument is always quoted as sovereign by those who seek to mitigate the decline (which cannot altogether be denied, and has not been by any serious critic). Readers, when they are familiar with all Conrad's books (and of course all of these, even *The Arrow of Gold* are of the greatest interest and merit – the decline is understood by all as being a falling-off from the great heights achieved by the best, by, most certainly of all, *Nostromo*) must read this for themselves and make their own decision. The Shakespeares of this world may or may not be free, as Arnold declared they were – but the common reader indubitably is. When any critic becomes an arbiter and forgets that he is himself a common reader, then he half-severs his connection with literature, and becomes an average professor or worse, something of a tyrant. The true critic can only offer his view in good faith – and this, the right disclaimers made, he ought untimidly to do.

Let me first give an outline of the argument for the decline, as it has been most effectively explained by Dr Bernard Meyer, author of what is probably the best psychoanalytical study ever made of an author – not the least because Meyer has good literary judgement. Meyer, who puts convincing emphasis on Conrad's psychic attachment to his mother, regards the illness of 1910 as an example of what he calls "Infection-Exhaustion Psychosis". This may sound like jargon, but what it means is this: a physical illness (gout) breaks out and reveals an emotional crisis which has long been in the making. Meyer rightly puts much emphasis upon the association with Ford. Meyer then writes (this passage is quoted by Karl, who wishes

– but with the utmost respect, since he owes much to Meyer – to refute it on account of *Victory*):

The most striking manifestation... concerns a pronounced shift in the moral and psychological orientation of his stories which is characterised by the exteriorisation of the source of suffering. As a consequence the poignant inner conflict of the early Conrad was replaced with conflict with the outer world, and doubting, troubled men, like Marlow of "Heart of Darkness" and hapless souls like Jim or Decoud, caught in a neurotic web of their own creation, gave way to simple creatures who, as pawns of fate, struggle with indifferent success against external influence, external accident, and external malevolence.

Meyer's argument maintains that, after *Under Western Eyes* and his breakdown, Conrad was no longer able to make the journey into his own unconscious which gave his earlier work its vitality and power: and it attributes this, not in any way unsympathetically, to Conrad's having adopted a means of defence against madness, which involved the phenomenon of "projection", i.e. Conrad viewed – and misinterpreted as reality – hopes, fears and wishes which resided within himself. So, Meyer concludes, Conrad, deprived "of that mirroring companionship [of Ford] which had sustained him in his earlier bold ascent... [became] ...a literary Captain MacWhirr", and cut himself off from the sources which fed his art. Thus, returning to an immature and unresolved Oedipalism (as one might put it, and as I think Meyer means) he began to have resort to "fictional females" who "unman" their victims: in other words, to *femmes fatales*.

I believe that this is essentially right, and most especially so in Meyer's superbly insightful phrase about Conrad's turning himself into a sort of MacWhirr. Of course, the argument can be over-simplified, and much could (and no doubt will) be added. A man who has had to turn himself into his own creation will often remember the joyous irony with which he created him – and may even resist being him from time to time with some success. Decline theorists do tend, as Karl complains, to make things too neat; but Karl himself, although (apparently) agreeing with Leavis's view of *Victory*, explicitly half accepts the decline theory. *Chance* is actually what most take it to be, "irritating": the nobility of Captain Anthony is as unconvincing as de Barral's meanness – the old edge has gone. The hinted at 'happy' ending is contrived, and Mrs Fyne hardly (as Karl rather surprisingly claims) represents a "step up" in "Conrad's conceptual powers" – he adds, with a donnish political correctness that Mrs Fyne "may reflect his greater awareness of women resulting from their agitation to gain the vote"!

I do not think that Conrad was ever quite as simple as that. The only comment he ever made on that issue was, in effect, "hurrah! It won't harm me!". Mrs Fyne, an utterly botched conception, fails because in her he was making a clumsy and angry double-thrust – at Ford and at his new companion Violet Hunt, a notorious agitator for the women's vote. He was thrusting at Ford by implying (as he clearly does) that Mrs Fyne was a lesbian. This is a classical ploy. The unaware homosexual – but let us say, here, the man in whom there is some 'unruly homosexuality', which he won't acknowledge, towards his male 'secret sharer', because the spiritual side of his sexual love for his wife has been frustrated by what we shall here describe as (nothing pejorative being intended) her 'stupidity' – projects his own feelings upon the man he loves. As I remarked, Conrad though no Freudian (he did not need to be), was not that simple, and so here he disguises Ford as his own mistress (of whom he is jealous and at whom he is therefore angry) and hints, but of course no more than hints ("if you say so – I'm admitting nothing"), that she is mannish (what could be more appropriate?), and lesbian (i.e. homosexual). She is Mrs *Fyne*, and what could be *finer* or more refined (especially with the 'i' transformed elegantly to a 'y' than Ford and his arty, born-into-the-pink manners? She is the daughter of a Pre-Raphaelite poet, Carleon Anthony, who wrote (my italics) "to glorify the result of six thousand years' evolution towards the re*fine*ment of thought, manners, feeling" (shades of Ford's ancestry). Ford's anonymous *This Monstrous Regiment of Women* (1913), a woman's suffrage pamphlet, had of course been written for (or with?) Violet Hunt. To make weight, there is the husband, too, the man called by Marlow "little Fyne": "an enthusiastic pedestrian", author of a book called *Tramp's Itinerary* (perhaps an allusion to Ford's *The Soul of London* and its two sequels – Ford had himself jokingly invented, in one of his novels, the perfect title for a Conrad book: *Clotted Vapours*): "Little Fyne held very solemn views as to the destiny of women on this earth, the nature of our sublunary love, the obligations of this transient life, and so on."

Conrad had written some of *Chance* before beginning "Ramuzov"; but when he came to complete it, he must have contrived it rather than go to all the pains of allowing it to come to its own conclusion.

Now to *Victory*, a better executed and more interesting novel. Guerard writes that it is "very badly written and very roughly imagined". That is carrying things too far. Conrad was trying to re-do *Nostromo* better, and is, as Karl rather incautiously says, "very much the conscious artist". He is too conscious, trying to imitate his unconscious (instead of delving into it for wherever it may direct him); and Karl's defence of the book is in fact extremely uneasy – "regardless of whether one feels he was successful or not", "no matter how we feel about the final version", and so on. This is a defence of Conrad the man, and of his courage and resolve, but not of his book.

The theme itself would have been worthy of Conrad at his best. Axel Heyst is an isolated man, having inherited from his cynical father an attitude of disillusion which he has not earned from his own experience. He leads an aimless existence, avoiding contact with people, or acting on impulse. He helps the captain of a trading brig, Morrison, by paying his fines – as a result he inherits a business. This fails, and he lives alone with his servant, Wang, on a Malayan island. But the Morrison involvement has consequences: Schomberg, a hotel keeper not unlike the Brown of *Lord Jim*, but more subtle and malicious, gives it out that Heyst killed Morrison for a fortune which he now has hidden on his island of Samburan. When Heyst 'rescues' Lena, a played-out English girl, from his attentions, Schomberg causes three villains to raid the island for the fortune. In the ensuing fracas, Lena is (accidentally) killed, and Heyst commits suicide by remaining in their bungalow while it burns. *Victory* has all the usual Conradian ingredients: is immensely professional, and a thoroughly good love and adventure story; its villains are far more lively than its heroes; it is also of the greatest interest as coming from Conrad; but the prose is flat and dilute by comparison with that of *Nostromo*, and the sexual relationship between Heyst and Lena is unconvincing, as is Lena herself. The title derives from this passage, describing Lena's death:

> The spirit of the girl which was passing away from under them clung to her triumph convinced of the reality of her victory over death… With a terrified and gentle movement, Heyst hastened to slip his arm under her neck. She felt relieved of an intolerable weight, and was content to surrender to him the infinite weariness of her tremendous achievement. Exulting, she saw herself extended on the bed, in a black dress, and profoundly at peace; while, stooping over her with a kindly, playful smile, he was ready to lift her up in his firm arms and take her into the sanctuary of his innermost heart – for ever! The flush of rapture flooding her whole being broke out into a smile of innocent, girlish happiness; and with that divine radiance on her lips, she breathed her last, triumphant, seeking for his glance in the shades of death.

For what must be a key passage, this is dreadful stuff, of which Conrad does not mean a word: he has gone back to the worst passages of rhetoric in *Heart of Darkness*; but there is no substance left, just the empty and tired words: "tremendous", "kindly, *playful*" (my italics), "sanctuary of his innermost heart", "flush of rapture", "divine radiance". He has gone to Dickens – but to the Dickens of Little Nell – with a vengeance! He never quite rid himself of rhetorical bad habits, even in *Nostromo*; but these are dregs of a style.

However, no reader of good heart can hold this failure – nor the relative shallowness of even later work – against him. He had given of his best, and had damaged himself so much in the process that we can applaud his courage in trying to keep on. But we must not be sentimental: it is his own best that supplies the standard by which not to be. The years of illness and toil had taken their toll, and Conrad had become tired. Even his criticism of other authors – so perceptive, as shown in his letters, that it could be collected into a short book – became less sharp. His reminiscences became laboured and rhetorical, rather than fresh as they had been in *The Mirror of The Sea*. Conrad aimed lower. In *The Shadow-Line*, he was still capable of genuinely moving work, rather than rhetorical conjuring. He had had it in his mind since 1899, when he wanted to try to discover the meaning of his own first command, in early 1888, of the *Otago* (at £14 a month, it is worth recalling). But by 1915 (he wrote the tale between February and December of that year – the 1916 of the "Author's Note" is an error) his intentions had changed. Inspired by the plight of his young son Borys (and the others like him), who had just been sent to France, Conrad now wanted to write an elaborate allegory in which his own most testing experience would provide a commentary – if only an oblique one – on the meaning of war. *The Shadow-Line* became the most exactly autobiographical of his works of fiction, for his narrative, while it does deviate from the facts in matters of the states of mind of some of the characters, does not do so in any very marked degree. Conrad was here trying to be realistic, and not to imitate his old self – of whose work he was, by now, simply incapable. In this case the essential truth, the faithfulness to his own perception, naturally hyperbolic (but not manipulative, as had started to happen in *Victory*) though this might sometimes be, was especially precious to him because of his feelings towards his son and about the disaster of war.

Through Borys he felt for "the others". As Jacques Berthoud claims, he "wanted to do his bit", and he could do that most effectively by reliving his own experiences when he crossed the twilit "shadow-line" between youth and adulthood. So it was the very act of writing that supplied the parallel to what Borys and the others were going through. Through his love for his son, he could negate his habitual feelings of black futility. By the art of hyperbole he saw into the hearts of those very men with whom, twenty-seven years earlier, he had served.

The book is dedicated to them, in a moving phrase: "Worthy of my undying regard." He saw into their souls: into the madness and weakness and confusion of the steward, into the conceit of Hamilton, into the courtesy and heroism of Ransome, and, above all, into his own, present, sincerity of purpose. That had not been with him as he worked at *Victory*. He was also able to give some kind of answer to the question that had always haunted him (and haunts most people): can we avoid our destiny? He himself never believed that we could. But a man can choose between the essential cowardice of an attempted avoidance of it, and a courageous and graceful acceptance of it. And in *The Shadow-Line*, because it is simple and because Conrad is not trying to re-do what he could no longer do, the rite of passage is a convincing one.

Just for once in his final fourteen years of writing, Conrad treats the theme of the 'supernatural' with honesty. He refuses to enter into the studious rationalism of a MacWhirr – that rationalism which so disingenuously underlies such a book as *Victory*. The narrator here records his "spiritual drowsiness", his concentrated feeling "that there was no wisdom to acquire". Later he would know that "one has to learn everything". But then a "strange sense of exultation began to creep over him; and later a

> sudden passion of impatience rushed through my veins, and gave me a sense of the intensity of existence as I have never felt before or since. I discovered how much of a seaman I was, in heart, in mind, and, as it were, physically – a man exclusively of the seas and ships; the sea the only world that counted, and the ships the test of manliness, of temperament, of courage and fidelity – and love.

This is plain, and it is sincere. Compare it with the purple passage describing Lena's death. This is simply a father who has been through his initiation offering a salute to one who is about to go through his; as such, it is moving enough, and is Conrad's true swan song, the final at its level – almost perfect work after *Under Western Eyes*. It was, as an admirer said: "truly worthy of him".

SELECT BIBLIOGRAPHY

Letters

Karl, R and Davies, L. (eds) *The Collected Letters*, 1983. Prints every known letter.

Biographies and Memoirs

Baines, J. *Joseph Conrad*, 1960. Critically inept, but still useful introduction; it was a worthy standard biography for many years.

Ford, F. M. *Joseph Conrad, A Personal Remembrance*, 1924. Idiosyncratic, but the key to Conrad from the one who knew him best. Totally indispensable for those who want to go into Conrad deeply. It urgently needs an annotated new edition.

Karl, F. *Joseph Conrad. The Three Lives*, 1978. Muddled and over-long, but still a valuable and suggestive study.

Meyer, B. *Joseph Conrad: A psychoanalytic biography*, 1967. An excellent and stimulating study, quite out of the general run of this (usually) dreary and silly sort of thing. The author has humour and good literary taste.

Najder, Z. *Joseph Conrad: A Chronicle*, 1983. Essential.

Sherry, N. *Conrad and his World*, 1972. The best start.

Tennant, R. *Joseph Conrad*, 1981. A good and sensible introduction. Readers could well begin with this after Sherry's briefer *Conrad and his World*.

Watt, I. *Conrad in the Nineteenth Century*, 1980.

Critical Studies

Berman, J. *Joseph Conrad: Writing as Rescue*, 1977. An interesting psychological study.

Berthoud, J. *Joseph Conrad: The Major Phase*, 1978. A dogmatic but provocative study.

Gordan, J. D. *Joseph Conrad. The Making of a Novelist*, 1941. The beginning, Morf's first book apart, of serious critical work on Conrad.

Guerard, A. J. *Conrad the Novelist*, 1958. A helpful, sensible and accessible study by a writer who is himself a novelist.

Kirschner, P. *Conrad: The Psychologist as Artist*, 1967.

Morf, G. *The Polish Heritage of Joseph Conrad*, 1930; *The Polish Shades and Ghosts of Joseph Conrad*, 1976. Two invaluable studies.

Moser, T. *Joseph Conrad: Achievement and Decline*, 1957. A major study of the decline.

Sherry, N. *Conrad's Eastern World*, 1966. *Conrad's Western World*, 1971. Psychologicaly often inept; in particular the author is blind to Conrad's irony; but his sleuthing is quite indispensable.

GREENWICH EXCHANGE BOOKS

STUDENT GUIDES

Greenwich Exchange Student Guides are critical studies of major or contemporary serious writers in English and selected European languages. The series is for the student, the teacher and 'common readers' and is an ideal resource for libraries. The *Times Educational Supplement (TES)* praised these books saying, "The style of these guides has a pressure of meaning behind it. Students should learn from that... If art is about selection, perception and taste, then this is it."

(ISBN prefix 1-871551- applies)
The series includes:
W. H. Auden by Stephen Wade (-36-6)
Balzac by Wendy Mercer (48-X)
William Blake by Peter Davies (-27-7)
The Brontës by Peter Davies (-24-2)
Joseph Conrad by Martin Seymour-Smith (-18-8)
William Cowper by Michael Thorn (-25-0)
Charles Dickens by Robert Giddings (-26-9)
John Donne by Sean Haldane (-23-4)
Thomas Hardy by Sean Haldane (-35-1)
Seamus Heaney by Warren Hope (-37-4)
Philip Larkin by Warren Hope (-35-8)
Laughter in the Dark - The Plays of Joe Orton by Arthur Burke (56-0)
Shakespeare's Non-Dramatic Poetry by Martin Seymour-Smith (22-6)
Shakespeare's Sonnets by Martin Seymour Smith (38-2)
Tobias Smollett by Robert Giddings (-21-8)
Alfred Lord Tennyson by Michael Thorn (-20-X)
Wordsworth by Andrew Keanie (57-9)

OTHER GREENWICH EXCHANGE BOOKS
Paperback unless otherwise stated.

English Language Skills *by Vera Hughes*
If you want to be sure, as a student, or in your business or personal life, that your written English is correct and up-to-date, this book is for you. Vera Hughes's aim is to help you remember the basic rules of spelling, grammar and punctuation. 'Noun', 'verb', 'subject', 'object' and 'adjective' are the only technical terms used. The book teaches the clear, accurate English required by the business and office world, coaching in acceptable current usage, and making the rules easier to remember.

98

With a degree in modern languages and trained as a legal secretary, Vera Hughes went from the City into training with the retail industry before joining MSC as a Senior Training Advisor. As an experienced freelance trainer, she has worked at all levels throughout the UK and overseas, training business people in communication skills, but specialising in written business English. As former Regional Manager for RSA Examinations Board, she is also aware of the needs of students in schools and colleges. Her sound knowledge of English and her wide business experience are an ideal combination for a book about basic English language skills.
ISBN 1-871551-60-9; A5 size; 142pp

LITERATURE & BIOGRAPHY

The Author, the Book & the Reader by *Robert Giddings*
This collection of essays analyses the effects of changing technology and the attendant commercial pressures on literary styles and subject matter. Authors covered include Dickens, Smollett, Mark Twain, Dr Johnson,; John Le Carré.
ISBN 1-871551-01-3; A5 size; 220pp; illus.

The Good That We Do by *John Lucas*
John Lucas's new book blends fiction, biography and social history in order to tell the story of the grandfather he never knew. Horace Kelly was born in Torquay in 1880 and died sixty years later, soon after the outbreak of the second world war. Headteacher of a succession of elementary schools in impoverished areas of London during the first part of the 20th century, "Hod" Kelly was also a keen cricketer, a devotee of the music hall, and included among his friends the great Trade Union leader, Ernest Bevin. In telling the story of his life, Lucas has provided a fascinating range of insights into the lives of ordinary Londoners: their entertainments, domestic arrangements, experiences of the privations of war, including the aerial bombardments of 1917 and 1918, and their growing realisation during the 1920s and 1930s that they were doomed to suffer it all again. Threaded through is an account of such people's hunger for education, and of the different ways government, church and educational officialdom ministered to that hunger. *The Good That We Do* is both a study of one man and of a period when England was changed, drastically and for ever.
ISBN 1-871551-54-4; A5 size, 213pp

In Pursuit of Lewis Carroll by *Raphael Shaberman*
Sherlock Holmes and the author uncover new evidence in their investigations into the mysterious life and writing of Lewis Carroll. They examine published works by Carroll that have been overlooked by previous commentators. A newly discovered poem, almost certainly by Carroll, is published here. Amongst many aspects of Carroll's highly complex personality, this book explores his relationship

with his parents, numerous child friends, and the formidable Mrs Liddell, mother of the immortal Alice.
ISBN 1-871551-13-7; 70% A4 size; 118pp; illus.

Laughter in the Dark – The Plays of Joe Orton by *Arthur Burke*
Arthur Burke examines the two facets of Joe Orton. Orton the playwright had a rare ability to delight and shock audiences with such outrageous farces as *Loot* and *What the Butler Saw*. Orton the man was a promiscuous homosexual caught up in a destructive relationship with a jealous and violent older man. In this study – often as irreverent as the plays themselves – Burke dissects Orton's comedy and traces the connection between the lifestyle and the work. Previously a television critic and comedian, Arthur Burke is a writer and journalist. He has published articles not only on Orton but also on Harold Pinter, John Osborne and many other leading modern dramatists.
ISBN 1-981551-56-0; A5 size 97pp

Liar! Liar!: Jack Kerouac – Novelist by *R. J. Ellis*
The fullest study of Jack Kerouac's fiction to date. It is the first book to devote an individual chapter to each and every one of his novels. *On the Road, Visions of Cody* and *The Subterraneans*, Kerouac's central masterpieces, are re-read indepth, in a new and exciting way. The books Kerouac himself saw as major elements of his spontaneous 'bop' odyssey, *Visions of Gerard* and *Doctor Sax*, are also strikingly reinterpreted, as are other, daringly innovative writings, like 'The Railroad Earth' and his 'try at a spontaneous *Finnegans Wake*'; *Old Angel Midnight*. Undeservedly neglected writings, such as *Tristessa* and *Big Sur*, are also analysed, alongside better known novels like *Dharma Bums* and *Desolation Angels*.
Liar! Liar! takes its title for the words of *Tristessa's* narrator, Jack, referring to himself. He also warns us 'I guess, I'm a liar, watch out!'. R. J. Ellis' study provocatively proposes that we need to take this warning seriously and, rather than reading Kerouac's novels simply as fictional versions of his life, focus just as much on the way the novels stand as variations on a series of ambiguously-represented themes: explorations of class, sexual identity, the French-Canadian Catholic confessional, and addiction in its hydra-headed modern forms. Ellis shows how Kerouac's deep anxieties in each of these arenas makes him an incisive commentator on his uncertain times and a bitingly honest self-critic, constantly attacking his narrators' 'vanities'.
R. J. Ellis is Professor of English and American Studies at the Nottingham Trent University. His commentaries on Beat writing have been frequently published, and his most recent book, a full modern edition of Harriet Wilson's *Our Nig*, the first ever novel by an African American woman, has been widely acclaimed.
ISBN 1-871551-53-6; A5 size; 295pp

Musical Offering *by Yolanthe Leigh*
In a series of vivid sketches, anecdotes and reflections, Yolanthe Leigh tells the story of her growing up in the Poland of the nineteen thirties and the second world war. These are poignant episodes of a child's first encounters with both the enchantments and the cruelties of the world; and from a later time, stark memories of the brutality of the Nazi invasion, and the hardships of student life in Warsaw under the Occupation. But most of all this is a record of inward development; passages of remarkable intensity and simplicity describe the girl's response to religion, to music, and to her discovery of philosophy.
The outcome is something unique, a book that eludes classification. In its own distinctive fashion, it creates a memorable picture of a highly perceptive and sensitive individual, set against a background of national tragedy.
ISBN 1-871551-46-3; A5 size 57pp

Norman Cameron *by Warren Hope*
Cameron's poetry was admired by Auden; celebrated by Dylan Thomas; valued by Robert Graves. He was described by Martin Seymour-Smith as one of... "the most rewarding and pure poets of his generation..." and is at last given a full length biography. This eminently sociable man, who had periods of darkness and despair, wrote little poetry by comparison with others of his time, but always of a high and consistent quality – imaginative and profound.
ISBN 1-871551-05-6; A5 size; 221pp; illus.

Shakespeare's Non-Dramatic Poetry *by Martin Seymour-Smith*
In this study, completed shortly before his death in 1998, Martin Seymour-Smith sheds fresh light on two very different groups of Shakespeare's non-dramatic poems: the early and conventional *Venus and Adonis* and *The Rape of Lucrece*, and the highly personal *Sonnets*. He explains the genesis of the first two in the genre of Ovidian narrative poetry in which a young Elizabethan man of letters was expected to excel, and which was highly popular. In the *Sonnets* (his 1963 old-spelling edition of which is being reissued by Greenwich Exchange) he traces the mental journey of a man going through an acute psychological crisis as he faces up to the truth about his own unconventional sexuality.
It is a study which confronts those 'disagreeables' in the *Sonnets* which most critics have ignored.
ISBN 1-871551-22-6; A5 size; 84pp

Shakespeare's Sonnets *edited by Martin Seymour-Smith*
Martin Seymour-Smith's outstanding achievement lies in the field of literary biography and criticism. In 1963 he produced his comprehensive edition, in the old spelling of *Shakespeare's Sonnets* (here revised and corrected by him and Peter Davies in 1998). With its landmark introduction, it was praised by William Empson and John Dover Wilson. Stephen Spender said of him: "I greatly admire Martin

101

Seymour-Smith for the independence of his views and the great interest of his mind;" and both Robert Graves and Anthony Burgess described him as the leading critic of his time. His exegesis of the Sonnets remains unsurpassed.
ISBN 1-871551-38-2; A5 size; 200pp

POETRY

Adam's Thoughts in Winter *by Warren Hope*
Warren Hope's poems have appeared from time to time in a number of literary periodicals, pamphlets, and anthologies on both sides of the Atlantic. They appeal to lovers of poetry everywhere. His poems are brief, clear, frequently lyrical, characterised by wit, but often distinguished by tenderness. The poems gathered in this first book-length collection counter the brutalising ethos of contemporary life, speaking of and for the virtues of modesty, honesty, and gentleness in an individual, memorable way. Hope was born in Philadelphia where he raised his family and continues to live near there. He is the author of critical studies of Shakespeare and Larkin and is the biographer of Norman Cameron, the British poet and translator.
ISBN 1-871551-40-4; A5 size; 47pp

Baudelaire: Les Fleurs du Mal in English Verse
translated by F. W. Leakey
Selected poems from *Les Fleurs du Mal* are translated with parallel French texts, are designed to be read with pleasure by readers who have no French, as well as those practised in the French language.
F. W. Leakey is Emeritus Professor of French in the University of London. As a scholar, critic and teacher he has specialised in the work of Baudelaire for 50 years. He has published a number of books on Baudelaire.
ISBN 1-871551-10-2; A5 size; 153pp

Lines from the Stone Age *by Sean Haldane*
Reviewing Sean Haldane's 1992 volume *Desire in Belfast* Robert Nye wrote in *The Times* that "Haldane can be sure of his place among the English poets." The facts that his early volumes appeared in Canada and that he has earned his living by other means than literature have meant that this place is not yet a conspicuous one, although his poems have always had their circle of readers. The 60 previously unpublished poems of *Lines from the Stone Age* – 'lines of longing, terror, pride, lust and pain' – may widen this circle.
ISBN 1-871551-39-0; A5 size; 53pp

Wilderness *by Martin Seymour-Smith*
This is Seymour-Smith's first publication of his poetry for more than 20 years. This collection of 36 poems is a fearless account of an inner life of love, frustration, guilt, laughter and the celebration of others. Best known to the general public as

the author of the controversial and best selling *Hardy* (1994).
ISBN 1-871551-08-0; A5 size; 52pp

PHILOSOPHY

Deals and Ideals *by James Daly*
Alasdair MacIntyre writes of this book: "In his excellent earlier book *Marx: Justice and Dialectic* James Daly identified Marx's place in and extraordinary contribution to the moral debates of the modern era. Now he has put us even further in his debt not only by relating Marx to his Aristotelian predecessors and to the natural law tradition, but also by using this understanding of Marx to throw fresh light on the moral antagonism between Marx and individualist conceptions of human nature. This is a splendid sequel to his earlier work."
ISBN 1-87155-31-5; A5 size; 156pp

Marx: Justice and Dialectic *by James Daly*
Department of Scholastic Philosophy, Queen's University, Belfast.
James Daly shows the humane basis of Marx's thinking, rather than the imposed 'economic materialistic' views of many modem commentators. In particular he refutes the notion that for Marx, justice relates simply to the state of development of society at a particular time. Marx's views about justice and human relationships belong to the continuing traditions of moral thought in Europe.
ISBN 1-871551-28-5; A5 size; 144pp

The Philosophy of Whitehead *by T. E. Burke*
Department of Philosophy, University of Reading.
Dr Burke explores the main achievements of this philosopher, better known in the US than Britain. Whitehead, often remembered as Russell's tutor and collaborator on *Principia Mathematica,* was one of the few who had a grasp of relativity and its possible implications. His philosophical writings reflect his profound knowledge of mathematics and science. He was responsible for initiating process theology.
ISBN 1-871551-29-3; A5 size; 101pp

Questions of Platonism *by Ian Leask*
In a daring challenge to contemporary orthodoxy, Ian Leask subverts both Hegel and Heidegger by arguing for a radical re-evaluation of Platonism. Thus, while he traces a profoundly Platonic continuity between ancient Athens and 19th century Germany, the nature of this Platonism, he suggests, is neither 'totalizing' nor Hegelian but, instead, open-ended, 'incomplete' and oriented towards a divine goal beyond *logos* or any metaphysical structure. Such a re-evaluation exposes the deep anti-Platonism of Hegel's absolutizing of volitional subjectivity; it also confirms Schelling as true modern heir to the 'constitutive incompletion' of Plato and Plotinus. By providing a more nuanced approach - refusing to accept either Hegel's self-serving account of 'Platonism' or the (equally totalizing) post-Heideggerian

inversion of this narrative – Leask demonstrates the continued relevance of a genuine, 'finite' Platonic quest. Ian Leask teaches in the Department of Scholastic Philosophy at the Queen's University of Belfast.
ISBN 1-871551-32-3; A5 size; 154pp

FICTION
The Case of the Scarlet Woman – Sherlock Holmes and the Occult
by Watkin Jones
A haunted house, a mysterious kidnapping and a poet's demonic visions are just the beginnings of three connected cases that lead Sherlock Holmes into confrontation with the infamous black magician Aleister Crowley and, more sinisterly, his scorned Scarlet Woman.
The fact that Dr Watson did not publish details of these investigations is perhaps testament to the unspoken fear he and Holmes harboured for the supernatural. *The Case of the Scarlet Woman* convinced them both that some things cannot be explained by cold logic.
ISBN 1-871551-14-5; A5 size; 124pp

MISCELLANEOUS
Music Hall Warriors: A history of the Variety Artistes Federation
by Peter Honri
This is an unique and fascinating history of how vaudeville artistes formed the first effective actor's trade union in 1906 and then battled with the powerful owners of music halls to obtain fairer contracts. The story continues with the VAF dealing with performing rights, radio, and the advent of television. Peter Honri is the fourth generation of a vaudeville family. The book has a foreword by the Right Honourable John Major MP when he was Prime Minister – his father was a founder member of the VAF.
ISBN 1-871551-06-4; A4 size; 140pp; illus.

104